Snakes in the Sass

Lynn Veach Sadler

Original title
Snakes in the Sass

Cover design
Sonja Smolec

Editors
Sonja Smolec
Yossi Faybish

Layout and Publishing
Aquillrelle.com

© Lynn Veach Sadler, 2011
All rights reserved

No part of this book may be reproduced or transmitted in any form or by any means, graphic, electronic, or mechanical, including photocopying, recording, taping, or by any information storage retrieval system, without the permission, in writing, from the publisher.

ISBN 978-1-105-21101-0

Snakes in the Sass: Contents

Backword [sic] 8

Garden of Punlips 13
Mr. Frost's Foul Fowling Piece 15
From the Quill 16
Dum, Dumer 18
The Promised Land 19
A Toast to Dame Nellie Melba 20
Dying on the Vine 21
Navel Lineage of The House of Tortellini 22
Staircase Wit in Jane Austen's House 24
Getting Down With the Emperor 25
Breakfast at Sea 26
The Uglies (For Mr. Darwin and His Progeny) 28
To Butterscotch and Butter Rum 30
The Child With a Good Book Takes to the Rook 32
A Child's Questions for the World at Large 33
The Girl in the Garden 34
Be Kind to Your Habitat! 36
Lobster Choice 37
Whale of a Cat Tale 38
Food That Rides Off into the Sunset 39
Art Is Just Too 40
Laughter at the Top of the World 41
Do the Gaza Strip 42
In Praise of "Juler Swan Dogs" 44
Flims Flams 46
Anthony and Cleopatra Have a Train-Love Tiff 47
Arkansas Traveler(s) 50
Art *Verb*alized 52

Buds Boys of the Summer Beach Make Do 56
Clickety-Clackety 58
Converting 60
Subversive? Yeah, Yeah, Yeah! 62
Beethoven *Appassionata* 64
The Biblical Railroad 66
Googores 67
Bird[er] in Closet Worth Many in Bush 68
Buying a *What* in a Poke? 70
Wool-Gathering 72
If You Would Bell the Cat 74
Flying Buttermilk Skies 76
Sea Cat 77
Battles of *Ac*t*i*um 78
Christmas Failures 79
Wild for Black Chicory Coffee 80
Misnomer 81
La Coiffeuse et La Voyageuse 82
Back Roads Nomenclature 84
Eschewing The Flat and The Dull 85
Of Ashes, Scraps, Scrapes, and Dirty-Word Stories 86
The Deck Autumn Deals 88
The Dogma of Poetry 90
Dry Bones Rise *Driza-Bone* Again 94
Apologia for The Dozens 96
Eagle on a Hot Tin Roof 97
Why Johnny Can't Equatorialize 100
EVA [Extra-Vehicular Activity] 102
When Flowers Play at Telephone [A Parody of Frost and "The Telephone"] .. 103
Feathers in Fortaleza's Cap 106

Gordian Knot Redivivus	108
Galahading and Galateaing	110
Hunter-Gatherer	111
Tale in Old Icelandics	114
Jour Maigre	116
All Dogs, Cats, and Fat-Cat Tourists Welcome in China: *Low*ku	118
Aristophanic Madang, Papua New Guinea	120
Mahla of Mumbai in Eden	122
Mickey Mousing	124
Of Lombok's Land-Bound Monkeys, Short-Tailed Cats	126
Leporidae in the Grass	128
Pique of the Moon	129
Feet Smart(s) in Granada, Nicaragua	130
Oh, Say, Can You *Sing* . . . ?	132
The Secret Life of Trains	134
Sheepish Over Ewe: Comeuppance to Apathy	136
Trolling	138
Love in Tulips	140
The Waits	142
All the Rage	144
Walking a Summer's Way	145
Purple Armadillos	146
Tourist Advisory for Yemen (and Parts Appertaining Thereunto!)	147
Beneath Meter; in Which the Lady Makes a Discovery	148
A Villanelle of the African [Non-]Violet	149
Ack-Ackery Chicken-and-Eggery, Or, Who's Flying Whom?	150
In the Land of *Oz*	152
Age-Marks	154
Batter (with Purple-Eyed Peas) Up!	155
Beating the Devil Running	158

Crashing in on His Spare Ball	160
The Genesis of "Don't Let the Bedbugs Bite"	161
Crabbing in	162
Memories Turned Legend	164
Ms. Age	165
Why God Chose Robert Frost over Elvis	168
Miss Austen Retorts	170
A Villanelle Against the Vilification of Grits	171
Why God Resorts to Private Journal	172
"*Who*-a—, *Who*-a—" for "*Wa*-tul-co"	174
Tuba Talk	176
A Villanelle Giving New Meaning to the Term "Old Dear"	177
The Lady Golf Pro, Having Heard It All Before, Turns *Golf* into *Flog*	178
A Sonnet Upon Asking My Students to Write a Sonnet in Class	180
On Sitting at the Back of Edward Albee	181
A Bray of Penguins; Being a Villanelleous Plea for Rehabilitation . . .	182
The Redemption of Noses in General, of My Nose in Particular	183
Antiseen, Antiheard, Antiwon	184
Not Birds of a Feather	185
Mr. Shaw and Mr. Churchill Correspond	186
A Villanelle of Vog	187
A Disquisition Upon Thatch on the Way to Jane Austen's	188
The Yankee Way	190
Flea Man, Flee Woman	191
A Villanelle Validating Tea Parties from One Who Has Been to Kenya	192
"Right" of Passage	193
Daughter of the Greenie Mother	194
Of Taste and Aftertaste	196
Fishing for Soul	198
Two-Tupping	200

Southern Showdown in New York 202
Toads in the Garden of Verse 203
A Cheesy Kyrielle 204
A Resolution Upon Pantyhose by the Right-Handed Woman 205
Hamlet in Las Vegas 206
When My British Friend Bayed, Paradoxically, for Mister Fox 208
Royal Flush 210
Barbie's Mother Calls Home 211

Mary Lynn Veach Sadler: Biography 215

Snakes in the Sass: Acknowledgments 219

Backword [sic]

When Aquillrelle Press approached me about submitting a volume of some two hundred pages of poetry for consideration, I blithely asked, "Anything you're particularly interested in? I've done 1100+ poems on many, many topics. War? World? Humor?" The immediate response was the last. Was this a joke? No one publishes humor! Hey, to bring out two hundred pages of *any* kind of poetry is amazing in its own right. Do these guys know I pass as a scholar and a Milton one at that? (Milton intimidates many.) Do these guys know I was a college president? You don't get by with much humor in that field either.

I'm married to the punster of punsters. When I told him I had to do this foreword, he said, faster than I could blink/think, "In this case of humor, you should call it a 'backword.'" So, a "backword" it is, *siced/sicked* to attest to my academic credentials.

Editors Yossi Faybish and Sonja Smolec begged a foreword in the belief that it will "help present the material to readers in the correct way." [Probably an oxymoron in there somewhere.] First then, a manifesto of sorts. I would not have survived some of my experiences without humor. I laugh often. When/*If* I can laugh, I'm free or on my way to being free. Second, I believe that words themselves have to be let out to gambol and leave would-be wordsters, gambling, behind. Words love to surprise, to be on their way to something else before their humans catch on. Third, I believe that no word is innately nasty [Hie you to Shakespeare!]; the nasty belongs to the voice and application of the user. Fourth, probably the major stinger, I always expect and want to learn something on the way to a poem/work, including the humorous kind. "Ah, but a [woman's] reach should exceed [her] grasp, or what's a [poem] for?"

My surprise here is the range. "Grouping" my work made me see it with new eyes. What I found is a sense of the different guises in which humor humors us. The collection has children's poems that aren't really for children, songs (ditto), stories from different points of view [I believe in personae.], the not-entirely-politically-correct [I've had to spend too much time being politically correct, and I am, after all, a playwright who has observed and *heard*.], subjects delved into [all you ever want to know about arts and crafts, I suspect] and learning (especially about tulips, Frederick Tudor of Nahant, Mickey Mouse), a healthy dose of formal verse tripped up by humor, some sad-edged humor [eschewing the flat and the dull], some ice-edged humor, age and youth, creatures, food, a bit of the bawdy if only of the "as the hearer hears" variety, telling by metaphor, limitations ("Yankee Way"), a bit at the expense of the great and the popular (Frost, Austen, the Beetles, Heston, Crash Davis, Elvis, Albee, Barbie) . . . .

Hey, overnight, roughly, I'm a "humor poet." My experience with this press has taken me from incredulity to delight—in its efficiency, agreeableness, willingness to "work with" . . . . To date, I've never had a better publishing experience. And that's no joke.

Snakes in the Sass

Garden of Punlips

If we could grow flowers like puns,
what a sepalous calyxy this would be!
What florescence! What efflorescence!
Pollination would never come cross,
and, at Christmas, all plants would wear anthers!

Pistil-Packing Mamas, in full bloom, full flower,
with late bloomers as a hedge,
wearing flowery petal pushers
with no nasty tares and, in season, widows' weeds,
would ply a weed-eating policy of hoe and sow.
Not a shrinking violet among them!
These garden plotters would need
no trowel and error, but would know
to grow after stamen and filament
until all the style was variegated hybrids
and the only stigmata, non-green thumbs.
Nor would we have to wait
until spring *icumen in*
for punlips to *lhude sing, cuccu.*

Not that life would be *all* edenic—
you could never enter a garden innocently,
for a petunia might bite you for your lack of wit.
And you might *miss* being led down the garden path,
for the only sinners here raise too much cane,
nip themselves in the bud, fail to talk in leaflets,
and try to stem their stock.

Even Ms. Camellia Bloomer,
though an intemperate relative of Amelia
and a potted planter in her flush and prime,
would never be allowed to fade upon the vine.
You'd never again be a plain old garden variety

or be arrested for stalking,
or get pinched in the bud,
and *this* primrose path would lead to *tell*.
No one would fall out of the punlips garden
except for exceeding snake in the sass.

Mr. Frost's Foul Fowling Piece

Mr. Robert Frost was quite in vogue
in poultry zines until he perched in print
that his friend John Hall,
who raised prize fowl, had geese
that roosted in trees even in winter.
Those farmer readers cried foul
upon the Frost-Hall fowl,
claimed no goose roosted in a tree
no matter the season or reason.
But Mr. Frost simply would not
fly down from his pride of perch,
went further out upon the limb
to honk upon the case.
"Geese would sleep out,
or float out, let us say,
where hens would roost in the trees.
To be sure. But what more natural,
in speaking of geese
in close connection with hens,
than to speak of them
as if they *were* hens?
'Roost in the trees' has here
simply suffered what the grammarians
would call attraction from the subject
with which it should be in agreement
to the one uppermost in mind.
That is all. But the idea
will have to stand, viz.,
that Mr. Hall's geese winter out,—
and that is the essential thing."
Frost, alas, was no longer essential
to hens, geese, yokels, or,
that most essential creature, his editor.
Mr. Frost, that brood of like feather fumed,
had laid a goose egg—ungolden.

From the Quill

Birds of literary feather
flock together,
not a whit afraid of being trite.

The Harlequin Ducks,
prolifically romantic,
host novel poetry slams.

Seeded by Merlin,
The Ancient Murrelet
waters whole slams with his rimes,

to which all present
try to drink in meter.
The Phalarope Patonly

comes too late each time,
frankly proclaiming
he doesn't like rhyme.

The Chipping Sparrow insists
upon playing golf,
has never made

the Grand Poetry Slam.
The Grosbeak is banned
for Hawking Bushtit and Wrentit.

(I, of course, quote!)
Other birds prefer
their prose refined.

Cooper's Hawk eyes writing
The Prairie Falcon with
"Deerslayer" molting into "Killdeer."

At the worst of times, Dickens wonders
why he didn't think of "Smew."
Forster's Tern, no fly-by-night,

touts *The Cinnamon Teal*.
The Raven feels evermore overflown.
Astride his nesting site, he perches,

sits, and nothing more.
If asked, he proclaims himself
more biblical than Crow

a full flood's age before E. A. Poe.
He'd like to ship out with Owl
(though afraid of Pussycat).

But when Spruce Grouse
offered to fly him off in *Spruce Goose*,
he promptly wrote *The Aviator*.

Still, all the pol parrots concur:
no poetry slam can ruffle feathers
like *The Parlement of Foules*.

Dum, Dumer . . . .

I do admire my English teacher.
She says the next best thing,
if you can't bring yourself
"to expose the self
in flesh or voice, as it were,"
is to do so secretly in writing.
Ergo . . . .

That last is an ellipsis.
Ms. Ellerby also swears by ellip*ses*.
She guarantees "ellipses keep
one's chestnuts from the fire."

Ms. Ellerby believes "verbalization
is the laxative of the soul."
Most adults would never think of
putting *verbalization* and *laxative*
in the same throat simultaneously.
They wouldn't know *verbalization* period.
Not even if it shouted at them.

Ms. Ellerby is always
making puns like that.
I guess it's catching.
You can see why most of her students,
even the dumb and dumber,
like Ms. Ellerby.

[Ms. Ellerby loved it
or seemed to
when I said I couldn't understand why
they didn't name that movie
or spell its name *Dum an Dumer*.]

The Promised Land

"It won't hurt. I promise!"
Thus speaks mother; father; doctor—
from your alpha to their omega;
minister, at the baptismal font before you're dunked;
teacher, of the upcoming test;
the venial of venery to virgins;
women, to the newly pregnant, about giving birth
(Some are slightly less promise-promiscuous:
"It may hurt just a little, but you'll forget it
the instant the baby comes. I promise!");
every aerobic and exercise guru;
ergo, LIFE (which feeds on promises).

We can muster variations on the theme:
"This is going to hurt me
far more than you. I promise."
"This is for your own good. I promise."
Thus speaks the spanker (more often father);
withholder of the request—parents and
relatives in general, mothers-in-law, teachers;
ergo, LIFE (which feeds on promises).

"I'll meet you. I promise."
"We'll spend time together soon. I promise."
"I'll help you. I promise."
"Everything will be all right. I promise."

I weary of being promisee.
The only way to keep promiser's feet to truth's fire
is to convert promis*er* to promis*or*
à la your attorney. In the meantime,
if you are to me once more promissory,
I promise to plunge from whatever promontory!

Snakes in the Sass

A Toast to Dame Nellie Melba

Dame Nellie Melba,
Helen Porter Mitchell as was,
ain't she now a something, Love!
Dame Nellie never
forgot her comings, Love.
Dame Nellie remembered our Melbourne,
now didn't she, Love.
That's what her dear "Melba" is for,
don't I reckon.

She was a wonder, our Nellie.
Even in that London's Convent Garden
(plain old *convicts* over here),
they calls her a—how is it?—
soprano—*Color-me*.
And *–tura*. *Colormetura*
(or something like).

She was in some big old *Rigginletto*
the swells all thought just grand.
Played this Lucy woman
on some English moor.

Such a peach she was,
they named her Peaches Melba.
But some chef 'e scoffed at her,
called her Melba toast.

Them toffs were all too ritzy
for our Nellie from ole Mellie.
If they come to Melbourne,
I'll fix their chops for 'im, I will.

Dying on the Vine

He was a landscapist by trade,
passed as an *artiste* in his profession.
She a Duke professor of Classics.
He a Southerner of North America;
she formerly of Emilia-Romagna.

He bedded her flowers, then her.
Breaking up their marriages?
Little more than sodding.
Didn't it renew soil, issue in new plants?

She spoke, unlike his dum-dum wife,
in tomes, of tomatoes.
He understood the gist of
poma amoris, love apple,
brought her a bushel from his garden
of thirty different kinds.

He was certain the Southern tomato's juice
would cure her recalcitrance of mind.
But, to his horror, she bit, spit out,
then tossed each kind,
scatting of San Marzanos, Romanellas
while taunting his tomatoes
with their kin—the nightshade family,
said he might as well feed her
belladonna, mandrake. Italian herbalists
were the first in the world
to describe the true genius of tomatoes.
Such was her claim.

His was that she was
a sun-dried-up Italian tomato
and certainly no plum.

Navel Lineage of The House of Tortellini

He was enamored of navels, he claimed.
"Look to the fair tortellini!"
Young women did not know
what he meant but loved his bravado.

He said he was an artist—of painting, love, and
lunches of tortellini. Yes, his Italian ancestry
simmered with, he said, cooks.
One had served *pampepato*

for a banquet of the Duke Borso d'Este.
Another had sent a *pampepato*
to General Eisenhower.
This swain further claimed

descent from Dante Alighieri
and the *faïence* makers of Faenza, Ravenna
(but would not say if Dante made lunch for Beatrice).
His "Look to the fair tortellini!"

lured and disturbed.
This was the very line and food
he fed to each of his many ladies for lunch.
One enterprising miss finally betook

herself on line and learned
the lineage of this swain's mystique.
She told all dames who would listen
of Ostilio Lucarini's play,

The Inventor of Tortellini,
about its cook who'd seen
the mistress of the household
sleeping in the nude through lunch.

So smitten was he
that his unrequited passion
issued in a paean of pasta
to her glorious navel.

Every day ever after, he served
the household tortellini for lunch.
This revelation did nothing to diffuse
the mystique of The Swain of Tortellini.

Staircase Wit in Jane Austen's House

It happened in Jane Austen's house, forsooth!
In Chawton Village, Alton, Hampshire rain.
(The rain perhaps explains why this deed came.)
The blackguard came into Jane's own bedroom.
He sidled up to touch my very arm.
"When we are home," he said, "will you have lunch?"

"Sir, I always eat lunch to help me grow.
I'm young, you know, and still don't have full growth.
Not tea alone? And what about your wife?
I like a heavy lunch. Does she also?"
I shook my brellie's drops upon him then.
"So sorry, Sir, perhaps you are too close."
He turned to flee my floods of rain and words.

I could have said, "You cad!" How'd he have felt?
He lacked both sensibility and sense.
A would-be Wickham wet and come to grief.
Not every woman's wanting mate, my man.
Miss Austen's readers, yes, think so, but that's
a common prejudice. I own more pride!
Now had you only Mr. Darcy been . . . .

Getting Down With the Emperor

I know you know
Hans Christian Andersen's
"The Emperor's New Clothes."
But I'll bet every piece
of every wardrobe,
you don't know the Emperor.
Penguin, that is.

Penguins go about upright
in black and white tuxedos,
but Mr. Emperor Penguin
is the largest penguin
you or I shall ever see.
As tall as your average
snowman/snowwoman,
he/she is the James/Mrs. Bond
of penguins, as elegant as tall.

Usually, that is,
for I have seen this
oh-so-refined penguin creature
slip-slide away,
at a pace remarkable,
upon its very belly.
It made me belly laugh!

Breakfast at Sea

Won't you please join me
for breakfast at sea?

If your seat's so low
your nose hits the roe,
sit on a whale spout,
lean on a slug's snout.

Who's our maître d?
An anemone!

Eggs laid by turtle
whose name is Myrtle.
We won't have to seize
our cheese overseas.
But you must decide
for whale on the side.

Seals serve from big plates
but don't issue dates.
Sea urchins beg crumbs.
(They're mostly all thumbs.)
Electric eels squeal,
doze, then have a meal.

Each of our courses
rides on sea horses.
Saddles of bacon
not to be shaken;
as sardines up-swarm,
porpoises perform.

In the crook you'll sail
of a mermaid's tail
when you dine with me.

What sights we shall see!
What foods we shall eat!
We'll feed the whole fleet!

The Uglies (For Mr. Darwin and His Progeny)

Name the ugliest-bodied creature you can name.
For most people, it's just a naming game,
(though every mother of them loves them).
Not so for Mr. Darwin.

Topping the list may be the poor warthog.
If so—quick!—get your thinking to unclog.
Ever so daintily the warthog tips.
Like the happiest child, it always trips.
How can such an animal be ugly?
(Even Mr. Darwin would admit,
it's not exactly snuggly.)

With the hyena, I've some trouble, too.
Better to laugh than its *ugly* to rue!
The snake that ins and outs its slimy tongue?
Pardon, please—it's just very high-strung.
Now flies the looming vulture. Triple yuck!
Had you really rather spy a lame duck?
In a while? Alligators! Crocodiles!
Ugly? Yes—
we don't wait to see their smiles!

And now we have the hellbender/
slimy salamander/snot otter!
Was Shakespeare's Juliet wrong?
Would this creature pass muster
with another name?
If it were purple?
You may escape parental rebuke
with just plain "salamander"—
but you'd better let the nomenclature
"hellbender-slimy-snot-otter" slide!
(Besides, bet you can't say that a fast five times!)

When, all squishy, squelched, and squashed,
road kill comes, don't "Ugh!"
Salute it with fee-fi-fo-fums!
Even the ugliest—the plug-ugly—
and I do not say so at all smugly,
can be treats—gratifyingly guggly.

Although I'd not be an ugly scolder,
ugly's in the heart of the beholder.
So join with Mr. Darwin
and all mothers—

salute the power of ugly,
especially as ugly advances
by dint of will to be different,
by clone or DNA, or by genius
of the brain that evolves
from DARWIN-PLUS-YOU.
Therein just may reside the secret of
every piggy creature's ambition
and will to survive.

Still, I will submit a question apposite
that Mr. Darwin forgot—
why doesn't ugly
evolve into its opposite?

To Butterscotch and Butter Rum

The red and green of peppermint
fade too fast to pasty white,
don't even give my tongue a tint.
Peppermint is rather trite.
The taste does leave a pleasant hint.
I would deign to take a bite.

No chump am I for chocolate!
Chocolate is much too dull.
It's not what you can use for bait.
Not that it's an obstacle.
I know a girl who ate a crate!
That was quite a spectacle!

Now Necco Wafers are good, too.
Pale pastels and powdered mist.
The licorice are just too few!
Hard to find, but don't desist!
For Necco Wafers, suck; don't chew.
Glad I am that these exist!

I growl if Gummy Bears are all.
Let them hibernate in spring!
I want my bears to stand up tall,
not to be a chewy thing
or turn my speech to creepy-crawl.
I, of course, except Ling-Ling!

When I am feeling somewhat low,
lemon drops are what I seek.
They'd make Snow White "Heigh-ho! Heigh-ho!"
Cheeks chipmunky—try to speak!
Oz-less, they're yellow, not rainbow.
Still, no lemon drop is meek.

But I love butterscotch and butter rum,
both so easy on the tum.
Fum-fo-fi-fee! Fee–fi–fo–fum!
Eef-if-of-muf! Fee–fi–fo–fum!
To butterscotch and butter rum!
To butterscotch and butter rum!

The Child With a Good Book Takes to the Rook

The child with a good book bests any rook
and never a castle for a book mistook.

The child with the book can visit a Chinook,
seek out any nook, eschew hook and crook.

The rook must all but straight lines overlook.
A rook never but rank-and-file overtook.

The child with the book can be king, queen—pocketbook.
Granted, better than pawn's may be rook's outlook.

The child with the book imagination undertook.
At most, the rook might fall in a brook.

If, hearing this, a rook feel shook,
the child with the book will get that rook off the hook.

The child with the book will look over the rook,
but never callously that rook overlook.
The child with the book might for the rook cook
and see that the rook of the cooking partook.

Honoring of the child with the book might this way look:
> "This child with the book betook
> to pursue the cause of the rook.
> This child with the book never any friend forsook,
> not even the lowly rook."

A Child's Questions for the World at Large

What does it mean
"to rain cats and dogs"?
What does it mean
"to go to the dogs"?
I think it's a nice place to be.
What's "canine" and "K-9"?
What's "curtailed," and why did
they laugh when I said it?
Why is the Tooth Fairy such a cheap skate?
(Or is she just what they call a "cheap *date*"?)
Why do they think I'm so smart?
Why does my balloon float away?
How do butterflies get in people's stomachs?
Why do days get so grey?
(Or why do they get so gr*ay*?)
What color is love?
Why does my mother know everything?
Why do people spell all the bad words
(just making me curious),
and then, when I guess,
get so furious?

Anyhow, I must be growing up
'cause I have all the questions—
and NONE of the answers!

The Girl in the Garden

I loved The Girl in the Garden instantly.
"You're talking to the flowers!
Watch yourself in the nosegays.
I gardened my garden yesterday
and was bitten by a petunia."

"Actually, the flowers were talking to *me*."

"What were the talking flowers saying?"

"That they talk all the time to people
worth talking to, that all flowers would
if we didn't make their beds too soft,
keep them sleeping,
that it's bad manners to talk first."

"That jostles something
in the garden of my brain.
It's . . . *Alice in Wonderland*?"

"Not <u>Alice's Adventures</u> in Wonderland
but *Through the Looking Glass*."

"Ah, *hare* of the Dodgson
that bit me as a child."

"Alice, rather, I think. She chased the—*rabbit*,
if you don't mind my saying so."

"White. With pink ears. And I believe
I'm chasing you, would give you un-birthday presents
365 days of the year, even on your birthday.
The flowers and I assess you
as a person worth talking to."

"And I you as
one who *jabbers wockyly*."

We were married two months later
in that same garden.

Be Kind to Your Habitat!

Environmentalists can get a life.
Nobody wants just now to trash the earth.
And Mother Nature's nudging Duncan Phyfe.
Brunei? Oil but no dearth of afterbirth.

Don't eat the animals! Don't skin the cat!
Don't raise your thermostat on poor wombat!
Biodegradable is where it's at!
Above all, be kind to your habitat!

Rock-eating air and acid rain went west.
And vog (volcanic smog) has one-upped fog.
On bigger-cat feet, vog climbs Everest.
The world loves prairie dog and polliwog.

Don't eat the animals! Don't skin the cat!
Don't raise your thermostat on poor wombat!
Biodegradable is where it's at!
Above all, be kind to your habitat!
Urbanely, nails urge non-Urban Decay.
They're colored "Rage," "Asphyxia," "Pigeon," "Bruise."
On wrinkles, sprinkle "Rain Forest Sachet"!
No hash from Syracuse to Vera Cruz!

Don't eat the animals! Don't skin the cat!
Don't raise your thermostat on poor wombat!
Biodegradable is where it's at!
Above all, be kind to your habitat!

Chagrin went out of *Vogue* with Ann Boleyn.
A model was caught dead in big cat's skin.
Don't eat the animals! Don't skin the cat!
Don't raise your thermostat on poor wombat!
Biodegradable is where it's at!
Above all, be kind to your habitat!

Lobster Choice

The lobster,
given a choice,
would probably have preferred ignominy.
As the shameful food of only the poor,
it was hardly harvested beyond limit.
But the Rusticators came in the wake of Thoreau,
determined to fathom Nature,
and fell upon the lobster as Rusticated food.
But how to have lobster when they weren't summering
(Nature-slumming, as it were)?
Lobsters were sent forth in dry smacks—
small vessels, usually sloops—
swaddled in seaweed and ice.
But, alas! Not even the poor would be caught
dead eating dead lobster!
Live lobsters were sent forth in *wet* smacks—
with holes in their hulls to let in the water—
no very satisfactory solution, as even
lobsterphiles might acquiesce.
Then the Civil War sanctioned canning,
and canning made war on the lobster.
The lobster's since been
bisqued, rolled, tailed, saladed, sandwiched,
McLobstered by McDonald's,
McMobstered,
McHighmuckamucked.
We, bibbed and tuckered,
fall on him fresh from the tank;
tucker him out
with cracks, sucks, and frothing cold beer;
belly up to his bier.
As you worship at the lobster's bier,
think how far he's come—
from the stomach of the poor to your own.

Whale of a Cat Tale

In Paris—true!—the Street of Fish and Cat.
Not *rue*, *poisson*, or *chat*. *En bon anglais*.
In humbleness, I give this caveat,
present to you the truth of this pathway.

A cat who claimed great fame came here to rid
Parisian quays of rats. His name was Abe.
"The Abe of Cats" would play all cats' El Cid.
Alas, as "Honest Abe," he was no babe:
"Of rabbits, rats, I tired; I wanted more.
When Jonah's whale came here, I had my fame.
I teased that whale until he walked ashore.
The fight was dire. Is not a whale big game?"

Puss wasn't "Abe"—his *pêche à la baleine*
was but a lowly fish from out the Seine.

Food That Rides Off into the Sunset

I've been warned by very wise people,
both literati and denizens of Grub Street,
never to write poems about food.
(At least the latter, I find quite remarkable.)
But, then, I've never taken a warning wisely, assuredly,
and have always been right full of beans.

So if I were to slip and write (right?) such a poem—
I'd indulge in MY FANTASY MENU, eat it right (write?)
back to a favorite time, place, and table.

Saloon Hour? *Gabby Hayes Roasted Peanuts,*
Cisco Kid Salsa and Pancho Chips
wet down with *Red Disturbance.*
"Happy Trails" Salad (Greens, Red Onion, Avocado,
Orange Segments, and "Ranch" Dressing).
Lone Ranger Mesquite-Flavored Steamship Round.
Mexican Spitfire Chicken Enchiladas.
Lash La Rue Sweet Potatoes (with "Whipped" Butter,
Cinnamon, Brown Sugar, and Secret Lillie Gilder).
Judge Roy Bean Pintos with Lillie Langtry Condiments
(Green Onions, Tomatoes, Green Pepper, Cilantro).
Cochise Corn Bread.
Smiley Burnette Blueberry Cobbler.
Eschewing greenhorns, I'd swap Steamship Round for
cattaloe, Texas longhorn, Sonora red, or zorrilla.
Entertainment? LILLIE LANGTRY,
THE FAMOUS OPERA SINGER
ADORED BY THE FAMOUS HANGING JUDGE,
JUDGE ROY BEAN.
Flowers? Plain "Jersey Lilies," no fancy fluff-duff.
Conversation? We'd chew on "op'ra house"
as the corral fence's top rail, where cowboys more or less
talked over the few things they talked over.
Benediction? *Adios, Amigos, until we eat again.*

Art Is Just Too . . . .

Some go gaga over Dada.
Tristan Tarzan, Hans Ape, Marcel Duchimp?
They mean going ape.
Cubists? Too more-than-two-faced.
Six-six-six-six-six-six! Too square.
Art deco? Too decorative.
Minimalist? Too little.
Miniature? Ditto.
Objet d'art? Ditto ditto.
Empaquetage? Too big.
Cave art? Too primitive.
Yamato-e? Art shouldn't tell stories.
Junk? Too garbagy.
Pop? Too canned.
Funk? Too California.
Gothic? Too Duke.
Japanned? Too cheap.
Pointillism? Ellipses running amok.
Kinetic? I do not want my art to fight back.
Figurative? I can look around and see.
Abstract? Never shows you a thing.
Collage? Just a collection of found things.
Psychedelic? Nobody's getting inside my head!
Moiré? Too wet.
Grotesque? Have you seen the new *Psycho*?
Biomorphic? Too hung up on Mother Nature.
Italianate? Mafia Dons?
Odalisque? Now you're getting there!
Nude? Mais oui! Make each one a *ten*!

Art? It's just too . . . all that jazz, I think.
Actually, I like
Playboy fold-outs best.

Laughter at the Top of the World

Well, now, if you insist upon living
in the Gar Hole of Despair
about the Human Condition,
I just may join
the Nanook family of the North.
The top of the world is not about to be
as cold as the Gar Hole of Despair.
Besides, I've been
even more than quite partial
to Eskimos since stumbling, dying,
frozen by your benumbing melancholy,
on the website with
Robert J. Flaherty's account of
making the first documentary about them.

When they weren't trying
to eat his gramophone records,
they loved hearing Jazz King orchestras
but burst out laughing and rolled on the floor
(or whatever igloos have)
every time he played Caruso as Pagliacci.
No flows of tears for the Eskimos!
(Or me.)

From now on, Dearest,
every time you leap into
that Gar Hole of Despair,
I shall respond "Iviuk! Iviuk!"
That's Nanook imitating the walrus
and my "Yuck! Yuck!" irritating you.

Do the Gaza Strip

Can't Arafat do the Gaza Strip?
Arafat won't let himself rip.
Is Arafat too fat to strip?
Now he's got that airstrip,
can forget statesmanship,
can't Arafat do the Gaza Strip?
Arafat is hip,
has to get a grip.
What a trip,
would make us all flip!

Know what Swift says about a Yahoo?
He didn't know Netanyahu!
Is Netanyahu Tribe of Dan?
He's not Mohammedan,
not a Vatican man,
won't read Koran,
fast for Ramadan.
Netanyahu's hip,
has to get a grip.
What a trip,
would make us all flip!

Will it hurt the world to know
Bilal Mosque is Rachel's Tomb?
Would such knowledge cause simoom?
It might make the desert bloom,
Sunni Muslims give up doom,
lift Middle East from gloom.
Our two guys are hip,
have to get a grip.
What a trip,
would make us all flip!

Why can't you guys just re-deploy!
You're both being so very coy.
Underneath, none of us is goy;
We are all hoi polloi!
Stop with being obese!
Do the Gaza Strip!
Please bring us peace!

When you two can't dance anymore,
Tel Aviv, Aziz, and Heimie.
Find a Golda, Little Egypt.
Tell them all: No more war!
Fa la! Fiddle–de–dee!
Do the Gaza Strip!
Strip or be Stripped!
Do the Gaza Strip!
Just let yourself rip!
Yes, Yasser!
Yes, Benjy!
Do the Gaza Strip!

I warned you:
you're dancing no more.
Our Ehud has stripped the Likud.
War hero Barak will force peace,
telling all: No more war!
Yitzhak Rabin is back
to Strip-dance again with Arafat.
Do the Gaza Strip!
Just let yourself rip!
Yes, Yasser!
Yes, Ehud!
Do the Gaza Strip!

In Praise of "Juler Swan Dogs"

Granddaddy Bob says, in his day,
dogs didn't have to stay penned up,
and during this running free,
young dogs would teach themselves treeing
by going after squirrels,
though squirrels weren't exactly
Top Dog in the Hunting World.
Still, if a dog had trained himself
to tree squirrels, you could teach him
to tree raccoons. It was mainly a question of
taking the dog out to Coon Country
to get him to see the error of his treeing ways.
All the same, Juler Swan, the local coon dog trainer,
did not want people to think
of his dogs as squirrelers
because he sold trained coon dogs
to folks all over the state.
Now, two of Juler's fourteen sons
have a website dedicated to
"Juler Swan Dogs" and sell all over the *country*.
In fact, they've even sold to
Saudi Arabia's Ruling Family
and came to see Granddaddy Bob
right after SEPTEMBER 11, 2001,
to ask him what to do.
Juler's descendants have gone big-time
into training "Juler Swan Dogs"
to hunt on desert sands
and not just for stray camels,
as you might expect, but for sand cats
and other desert creatures
and, most important, for underground caves
where terrorists hide out.
The Bin Ladens wanted to be sure that,
when they disowned Osama,

he had to take his network elsewhere.
"Old Juler Swan's boys"
wanted to know from Granddaddy Bob
how to offer their services
to our forces in Afghanistan
without getting accused
by the FBI, CIA, and ALL AMERICA
of having aided and abetted
the Taliban and al Queda Network.

The Swan boys have taken
these Ugly Duckling dogs
and taught them to follow
sand ripples or "pistes,"
soothe camels so they won't run away
and will feel better about how they look,
and warn of impending simooms,
dustdevils, sandstorms,
scorpion attacks, etc. Best of all,
these "Juler Swan Dogs"
survive by drinking camel spit,
and probably humans will learn from them
how to do so in the next few years.
Granddaddy Bob was helpful,
though opining that Juler Swan Dogs
and Juler Swan Boys had "*piste* him off."
Granddaddy Bob says, if Juler Swan's boys
have learned to say *piste*,
they ought, at the very least,
to go for *sputum* or *expectoration*,
and *whom* are they trying to *phlegm*-flam?

Granddaddy Bob also says "Juler Swan Dogs"
deserve credit as the
"only ones left in America
who'll still 'walk a mile
for a Camel'!"

Flims Flams

My best friend Doak just saw *Bones*,
which has a dog that projectile-vomits
thousands of maggots.
He went because
Snoop Dogg is the star, but I think
he was fascinated with the dog scene.
I plan to stick to Snoop Dogg's music.

I did like *A Nightmare on Elm Street*
and the *Friday the 13th* flicks, though.
I guess they're *flims flams*,
but I like them.

Flims flams is a great pun,
but you have to be in the know.
I taped *City of Joy*
to watch with Granddaddy Bob.
Not only is it a great movie,
but the Indian kids in it
who moved to the big city
want more than anything
to see "flims."
After seeing *City of Joy*,
I've taken to referring to
bad movies as "flims flams."

Anthony and Cleopatra Have a Train-Love Tiff

"You never talk to me anymore, Anthony.
We're like two trains passing in the night.
Our heyday of steam has passed.
In our salad days . . . ."

"All these waybills, Cleopatra!
Our budget's a runaway train."

"Why, we could inspect, clean the fire of,
coal, sand, water, and turn
132 engines every twenty-four hours."

"Back-track that, Cleopatra!
We need to make a watch comparison."

"Oh, Anthony, you decapod!
You're so square you can't circulate
except in a roundhouse.
But you did have such a line,
and we did make some
beautiful white smoke together . . . ."

"And you were always running trackside.
Now, I see you only at the bottoms of cuts,
through a tunnel darkly.
You're no longer trackside, Cleopatra."

"All my tractive effort goes just to
keeping the home fires stoked, Anthony."

"Your unhappiness is driving a spike
in my heart, Cleopatra.
But you spend so much time and money
on that fancy hardware!
Then you go wig-wagging away in them
like some magnetic flagman.

Every man with any iron in his soul,
the mighty Julius Caesar included,
has to stop and ogle,
and I go crazy jealous, Cleopatra.
You have such a high-riding boiler
and such a fine cylinder saddle,
and your plate and cold frame
are so . . . incredible.
Must you buy those clothes that
show so much daylight above your wheels?
What if I start greasing my wheels again
over my wife Octavia?"

"Great billows of steam!
You'll find asps in your basket!"

"No need to blow a gasket!"

"Let me get my hand on the
lanyard of a water tank,
and I'll douse *your* white-hot firebox fast.
Here's a turntable right enough,
and I do not intend to be
your merry-go-round—
or your bridge sidings either!
What are you
lubricating your rods about?
I've begged and begged you to
stay out of the lubritorium.
Who gives you all these
'proceed!' train-order signals?
It's enough to send me
after you with an alemite gun!"

"Five years with you and I feel
like my boiler's busted and
my water tank's rusted."

"And *me*? I've known
the world's biggest trains!"

"That's enough to make me
impale myself on a cowcatcher."

"Oh, Anthony, don't enginate on me!
You just need to be
anointed with a little oil.
It's back to the lubritorium for you.
You'll make the grade.
No detraining in sight.
I didn't mean any of those mean things."

"Nor did I, Cleopatra!"

"Oh, Anthony, you *are*
worth your cinders.
May the gods of Egypt *and* Rome
bless your cinders every one."

Arkansas Traveler(s)

More legerdemain than legend.
Such a tangled tale.
Who did what, said what?
(Who *played* what, for that matter,
and *who* wrote what was played?)

Was the Fiddler the Traveler
and vice versa?
Why was *The Arkansas Traveler*
a hit play in Ohio anyway?
Did Colonel Faulkner get the credit

so Arkansas could give Mississippi
a run for its writer legends?
I cannot grasp
the anacoluthics of this legend.
But I have thought considerably upon it,

dug and dug, and here is what I think.
This is another case of Arkansas
practicality versus country cunning.
Now the traveler is from Arkansas
and wants to dwell in practicality.

He should have known
the old man in the cabin
playing in the rain
had made a pact with Old Nick
for his playing prowess

and could not put by his bow.
But our fanatical fiddler
cannot admit his plight to the traveler.
Rather, he hardscrabbles
country wit into cantankerosity.

Who can mend a roof
upon a rainy day?
What cabin leaks
when it doesn't even rain?
I realize my resolution

begs the question of
musical improvisation, and,
having thought considerably upon
this arcane Arkansas conundrum,
I find myself in a high tuckahaw.

I'm moving on
to "Turkey in the Straw."

Art *Verb*alized

Art everythings and anyones:
Acts, proacts, pantomimes, whittles,
carves, knits, draws.
Artfuls, paints, sings, dances,
writes, oboes, guitars.
Westerns, jigglers-Jell-O,
Julia-Childs, clowns, comics.
Creates, theorizes, dares,
is-almost-always-on-its-arsis.
Still-lifes; still lives; *Ars longa*ses.
Grandma-Moseses, Picassos,
Beardens, occasionally Tahitis.
Trains, tracks, locomotives,
Baldwins-*Tell-Me-How-Long-the-Train's-Been-Gone*,
Seagals-"After-the-Train-Has-Gone."
Mysteries, mystifies, skates, universalizes,
"Wows!", "Gee-whizzes!"
Stencils, collages, water-colors, cloisonnés.
Births, surmises, thinks, opines,
definitively defines, absolutely
abstracts. Escapes, seascapes,
landscapes, mindscapes.
*La-Frontera*s, converts-douaniers,
sometimes-Christianizes.
Colors, unblushes, inclusives,
Clint-Eastwoods. Surprises, adorns,
embosses, kindles-fire.
Ideas, embouchures, embroiders, embraces.
John-Fords, John-Waynes, musical-theatres.
Tropes, emcees, emendates, empathizes.
Emphasizes, humanizes, tantalizes, socializes.
Keepsakes, fascinates, articulates,
adumbrates, advantages.
Educates, buhls, gardens, contemplates.

Asks-"What-if-we-did . . . ?",
"What-if-we-didn't . . . ?"
Continuouses, documents, discusses, declaims.
Deckles, art-decos, convinces,
joie-de-vivres.
[Ap]proves, hospices, huzzas,
hallelujahs, hosannas,
heals, heals, heals.
Flowers, elucidates, unites,
lucubrates, enlivens.
Silhouettes, longstands,
pax-vobiscums, wart-hogs.
Ogden-Nashes, does-alls,
hurdy-gurdies, carousels.
Energizes, enriches, emblazons,
transfixes. Eameses, Ehles,
Minnie-Evanses, transforms, awes,
occasionally-adolesces.
Heroes, tames, soothes,
shocks, therapeutics.
Sibyls, liberates, Scheherazades,
occasionally preaches.
Yarns, fables, barnyard-tales,
tankas, epics.
Suffers-(quietly),
sheds-its-tears-in-amber,
occasionally-lands-in-prison.
Greeting-cards, posters, *does*,
but-*does-not*-posture.
Pianos, every-instruments, goods, enhances.
Moods, struts, sculpts,
pietàs, doodles.
Operas, arias, glissandos, passacaglias.
Disarms, alarms, warns,
fathoms, peaces, pieces, wars.
Models, sceneries, aligns,
captures-(yet-takes-no-prisoners).

Eases, easels, marbles,
marvels, oils, rubs-brass
(is-never-brassy). Computers.
(Does clip-art?)
Renaissances, renaissances,
"Nude-Descending-a-Staircases."
Fine-arts, folk-arts, finesses,
needlepoints, ceramics, effervesces.
Viscerals, virtuals, toles, etches,
weaves, baskets, enamels, knows,
nohs, haikus, sasses.
PUNs, possesses, purls,
pearls, pasts, nows,
futures. Origamis, sumies, seasons,
bonsais, dolls. Fabergés,
encourages, jazzes, line-dances,
ballets. Plays, plays-right,
playwrights, celebrates, Washi-eggs,
offers, sonnets, elegizes.
Madonnas, angels, angles,
guards, guardian-angels.
Touches-with-class, reminisces,
preposesses, smocks, tailors.
Sacreds, profanes, quilts,
reflects, hears, audiences.
Wall-hangs, carpets, floors,
wraps-babies, reads, interprets, poets.
Beauties, literatures, dramas,
palettes, Campbell-soup-cans.
Oldveaus, nouveaus, volunteers,
fugues, fiddles, violins.
Beads, petit-points, laces,
clogs, counts-cross-stitches.
Derives, enlarges,
builds-on-the-backs-of-giants.
Entertains-angels-[un]aware,
Bibles, blesses-interlopers.

Papier-mâchés, tapestries, macramés,
tap-dances, silks, corn-husks,
wreaths, drolls. Builds-bird-houses,
crafts, stages, simples,
complexes. Glissades, graces, tunes,
crescendos, études, adores.
Gives, feeds, sustains, succors,
chefs. Serves, preserves, complements,
compliments, accompanies. Arranges,
costumes, movies, films, NPRs,
PTVs, classics, concertizes.
*Eyre*s, plain-*Jane*s, raises-the-Dickens,
Beats, Jarrells, Langston-Hugheses.
Sews, histories, photographs,
phonographs, Cds, aesthetes.
Takes-athletes-to-higher-levels, evens-
playing-fields. Nurtures, cultures,
childs, adults, middleages,
Middle-Ages. Roars, leads, guides,
steers, politics, scherenschnittes.
*Paradise-Regained*s, McCullers,
Blues, Greens,
Betts, Prices, Faurés.
Sows, reaps, mends, mirrors,
calms, exhibits, performs. Grows, OPs,
Pops, Rococos, x-ray-paintings.
Waxes-(never-wanes), occasionally-
works-underground.
Teaches, lives-(never-dies), laughs-(never-lies),
occasionally-lingers-underground.

Congregates, collaborates, conjugates/*is*—
    I talent . . .   We talent . . .
    You talent . . .   You talent . . .
    He, She, It talents . . .   They talent . . .

Art everythings and anyones . . .

Buds Boys of the Summer Beach Make Do

After Bubba stole the Dodge pick-up
from the father of another Bud, Jessie-P,
who lived at the beach year-round,
we Buds Boys of the Summer Beach
had to "make do."

It was pushing midnight, and Bubba
was high and trying to strip the gears
while he played the radio to its max.
Maybe if the music had been
purer country-western,
matters would have gone better,
but The Band was offering
"The Night They Drove Old Dixie Down,"
and it stirred the blood of all non-Yankees
up to two islands away, including Jessie-P's daddy,
the local police, owners, and renters.
All the Buds who could "pack" into cars
(with six packs "in tow") joined the chase.

The beach would have lost all its dunes
sans benefit of hurricane if most of Bubba's
motorcade hadn't stalled in the sand.

Bubba would roar past the cars
straining to dig themselves out
and give the well-known sign of engagement,
yowling his screech-owl laugh and yelling,
"Suck hind tit, Boys! This Dodge can dodge
anything you've got!"

Our secret name, "Buds Boys of the Summer Beach,"
made the papers, and even the "good ole boys"
tarred us right along with Bubba.
The best we could do for ourselves after that

was to chip in to buy an old Nash Rambler
and cut it down for a beach buggy.
To make our case with Bubba,
who loved big-time sports car racing,
we wouldn't let him go with us
to Marlboro and Sebring that year.
He was chastened but never ceased
to champion Dodge pick-ups.

Clickety-Clackety

Automobiles have come of age.
Click and Clack, the Tappet Brothers,
named themselves for the clickety-clack
of aging autos, whose drivers
sport jet lag like boutonnieres
but choke at any mention of "valve lash."

Tom and Ray have taken
cars and *Car Talk*
to the highest level
short of heaven—
to National Public Radio
and Penguin Putnam for print.

Even New Yorkers who don't drive
listen to these MIT grads
who sound just like them.
Why, the Magliozzis could be
invited to New Jersey to sing on
The Sopranos! My car volunteers
to escort them.

And how these bros have evolved!
From the do-it-yourself
of "Hacker's Haven,"
they've driven on up
to the "Good News Garage."
Click and Clack have made cars fun!
"And *funny*!" my car says.

The only trouble is,
my car insists on pulling off to listen
when Click and Clack come on NPR.
Its favorites of their lines
are "The Hatchback of Notre Dame"

and "Born Not to Run"!
It laughs so much,
it's getting clickety-clackety
before its time!
But I accept this as *good* car news.
When a car can laugh at itself,
you're almost home.

Converting

Once in a while, I like to dream of being "it"
in a "Vette," "Ain't she cute!" in a "Corvie,"
holding the world at bay in my Sting Ray.

Once in a while, I'd like to shake up/off my nerd
behind the wheel of a Thunderbird.
Please call me "Mustang Sally," "*Queen* of the Road"!

But now is true confessions time:
I can't pronounce *Jaguar*
with three-syllabled British bray.

I don't do stick shift (only safety belts).
I never found Paradise by dashboard light,
jerry-rigged a hot rod Lincoln.

Still, I like the thrill in dreams
of drag racing and street-cruising
(or being street-cruised upon).

I'll never be James Bond to cars
(more likely, Nancy Drew).
And all my dream cars have, alas,

converted to car dreams.
But "bulgemobiles" are driving out,
though Hummering, as hybrids come rolling in.

And I'm not entirely bereft—
I write wishes in the big-car dust.
Recently a friend took me for a ride

in her not-for-sale black Pontiac Solstice,
and did we swivel necks
(not to mention all our hair)!

Please honk for this
one last confession: in my dream that night,
I converted said convertible to red!

Subversive? Yeah, Yeah, Yeah!

If Lyndon had let them in the White House—
"Please please me," Luci Baines pled—
would he have been victorious in Vietnam?
It was a hard day's night; Lyndon had to yelp "Help!"
He was not Maharishi Mahesh Togi.

Subversive? Yeah, yeah, yeah.
All those little ole ladies taken in by
"When I'm Sixty-Four,"
all those mean-men Southerners trading in
liver pudding for Liverpudlians,
Dr. Peppers for *Sgt.* Peppers.

Subversive? Yeah, yeah, yeah.
Why did parents, parents' parents pretend
you were the Scourge of Hell,
corrupting sweet young daughters?
They forgot "Moonlight Swoonatra"
rubbing against the microphone
while bobby-soxers swooned,
all those sweet young "Sinatratics" throwing
bras and panties at Frankie Boy.
Subversive? Yeah, yeah, yeah.
Parents can be subversive.

Lennon just had to quip the Beatles were
more popular than Jesus.
We wanted to trade in Paradise for Pepperland.
"Burn, burn, burn everything that's Beatle!"
Puff the Magic was the *Grand* Dragon then, and
"Tomorrow Never Knows."
You Beatles let the world think Paul dead.
Somebody got John, helter-skelter, with
Charles Manson.
The Heart of Darkness, Man, Big-Time.
John Lennon was the "Nowhere Man."

Subversive? Yeah, yeah, yeah.
Yesterday and Tomorrow can be subversive.

God put "John in the Sky with Diamonds."
And God said, "Hey, Dudes,
Jude was my brother first!"
God's *Magical Mystery Tour* still hasn't failed,
and Some of His still go via *Abbey Road*,
where "All You Need [They Say] Is Love."
Now you may want to hold His hand,
oh, yeah, yeah, yeah.

The Beatles knew you "Can't Buy Me Love,"
not until you "Twist and Shout"—
for which we're now too civilized,
even were we to see
Eleanor Rigby herself Standing There
with the Queen Mum in all their glory,
and Princess Di right on the left.

Beethoven *Appassionata*

The sublime prodigy,
Beethoven of Bonn,
rebelled first against his father,
then against the world.
He cared not a fig for rules;
could not be taught;
knew his own genius;
composed slowly,
with an unemptied chamber pot
beneath the piano
(though he railed against
composing at an instrument).
The Baron de Trémont experienced
the chamber pot.
Did the chamber pot portend
the great chamber music?
Did the thunder mug
give rise to the railing?
Servants would not serve
tantrum-given Ludwig van,
who railed at his nephew Karl;
smashed pianos,
begging manufacturers for better instruments.
What was in Beethoven's heart must out—
music or passion for women.
Unattractive, *Der Spagnol*
for his swarthiness,
clumsy in all but music,
he was yet beloved by women
and aristocracy.
A revolutionary, he would not abide
Buonaparte's declaration of Emperorship,
ripped apart the dedication page to the *Eroica*.
A great pianist,
greater improviser.
A man of absolute pitch.

He belittled Haydn,
Mozart's manual air-sawing;
damned *Don Giovanni* for an immoral plot!
His rages raged before his deafness.
The Heiligenstadt Testament,
addressed to his brothers
to be read after his death,
laid responsibility for
his "personality" to his infirmity:
he could not admit frailty in the one sense
that must be more perfect
in him than in others.
His orchestras learned to look at first violinists.
He died during a storm.
At a final flash of lightning, clap of thunder,
the dying Beethoven raised up and shook his fist.

The Biblical Railroad

Like Andrew Carnegie, though that's about
the end of the similarity, my daddy
started out as a railroad telegrapher.
Even after he became a stationmaster
for the Raleigh & Augusta Air Line,
he never lost his fondness for telegraphy.

Daddy used to telegraph Bible verses
in Morse Code to my brother Ben and me,
was none-too-pleased with our translations.

Now Daddy, naturally, didn't send
us verses like "Jesus wept."
And that man was a stickler for details.
He telegraphed us—I can hear the clicks now.—
"And the Queen of Sheba came to Jerusalem
with a very great train." Daddy was
powerful upset when we got one
tiny little preposition wrong
and read back that the Queen of Sheba
"came to Jerusalem *in* a very great train."
Till Daddy set us straight,
we thought the Queen of Sheba
was the first lady railroad engineer!

But I heard him laughing
when he told Mama about it.
Daddy said it was a fine example of
"*train*ing up a child in the way he should go."

I later discovered that railroads and the Bible
had worked together before Daddy.
The Vermont legislature ruled that trains
could run on Sundays—if the conductors
read scripture to the passengers.

Googores

The British staid?
I was amazed.
The Oxford lecturer on the ship—
not quite a "don," but he'd attended—
was a Brit but droll.

If only we would go
"right the way round" and "in good order,"
and if only there is
no "subsidence of the road,"
"distances being what they are,"
"in the fullness of time"
(his favorite expression),
we'd not need "parapluie,"
could make our "brellies" "parasols."

"In the fullness of time," he assured us,
"hey, presto!" things would "come right"
and all before "Prince Albert
popped his clogs."

"In the fullness of time,"
all would be "whacking great,"
"absolutely spot on!"

The British staid? Not so!
It's "Fanny's Auntie
up your drawers!"
It's "right way round"
and all "googores."

From all of which, I do infer,
the British are our "rellies."

Bird[er] in Closet Worth Many in Bush

Welcome to Brisbane, Australia's Lamington National Park—
with O'Reilly's Guest House just at its heart
and the lushest green rainforest.

Ah, animals at last!
I pant for pademelon, potoroo, platypus—
oh, even the everyday possum—
it's said to come ring-tailed and brush-tailed here.
I wince for our hairless-, straight-tailed kind,
embarrassed by my betrayal.
But, next to Africa, Australia is the land for animals!
Australians drink "koala," "roo" the day.

We arrive at O'Reilly's late, go straight to our rooms,
are up at five for our first "Nature Walk."
The tourists are chirping, cawing,
clawing for (mostly video) camera space.
The word "bower" flies through the air
like some awesome pterodactyl.
I'm ready to bet that the pademelon lives
in a pretty bower . . . . One of the Clan O'Reilly
holds forth about bright baubles in the bower . . . .
I can't concentrate on *in the bower* because I'm being
beset by—bright baubles *in the air*.
They seem to be coming closer.
I *will* myself to act like all the bold birders about me.
(Accustomed to birds behind, occasionally *under*,
glass, I hope for *life*, not *life list*.)
They land on my head and others'.
They're *what*? Parrots? Parrot-bright anyhow.

The days at O'Reilly's are birdful:
the birders are constantly aflutter,
insist upon sharing their sightings with me:
pied currawongs, rainbow lorikeets,
glossy black cockatoos, crimson rosellas

Snakes in the Sass

(though I dasn't say so,
I prefer the orange of Adelaide),
king parrots, spine-tailed log runners . . . .
The birders look at me strangely
when I prefer the brush turkey—
and leave me to my own birding,
particularly when I whisper, ever so nicely,
"Don't you agree that our guide
should come out of the closet as a b-i-r-d-e-r?"

Buying a *What* in a Poke?

I listen carefully to the local guide,
tacitly agree that
Lunenburg is quite lovely,
this fishing capital of Canada,
with the largest fish plant in North America,
the second largest in the world!
I'm a bit skeptical of
the five-sided *Scottish* dormers,
this being the oldest *German* settlement
on our continent, but properly appreciate
the famous "Lunenburg bump,"
all other accoutrements
of the "paycheck houses,"
like learning the difference between
widow's and *captain's* walk,
eat the "mug-up" with relish—
the Solomon Gundy and Lunenburg Pudding.
I'm pleased to hear and see Edison Tanner—
he's eighty-three—at the carillon
in the Lunenburg Anglican Church,
am amused (but slightly superior)
as the superstitions are summed.
It's bad luck to bring coffins through the door;
Lunenburgers have special coffin windows.
The Devil enters through the back door;
Lunenburgers copy the fronts
of their houses at the back.
Never pass anyone in a stairway.
Sweep your store from front to back
to bring the customers in.
Don't permit suitcases or ladies on board.
Never say but always spell it—
p-i-g. Better yet,
refer to p-i-g as "Mr. Gruff" or
"Mr. Dennis" or plain old "curly tail."

What did that guide say?
I'm from the *pork* capital of the world!
Why, my daddy . . . .
I press the issue closely, stalling his spiel.
He's sorry, but he just doesn't know why,
something to do, he thinks,
with the ability of the p-i-g
to whistle up a wind.
"But there's p-i-g in
your Lunenburg Pudding," I exclaim,
trying to bring all *Looney*burgers
to their senses.
"And this place is German—
it can't be biblical,
this porcine prejudice!"
That little p-i-g
I had the good sense to make stay at home,
but my next little p-i-g
I sent straight to the Lunenburg market:
"Would you buy a p-i-g in a poke?
Why, it's compounding the folly!"

I muttered "p-i-g, p-i-g, p-i-g"
all the way home.

Wool-Gathering

The camelids, except the camel,
should claim kin with cats.
They are aloof, aristocratic, undomesticated.
All of them, including camel, spit in great disdain.
All ruminate—upon the world (and cud).
All wool-gather.
If you use the camelids for fuel,
the reason is,
they let you have their leavings.
No camelid will carry you, though
it might, to hone its sense of balance,
flagellate, or immolate,
accept a modicum of cargo.
Camelids live in their own Camelot.

The Andean camelids are all high-born.
The wildest (*highest*-born), guanaco,
swims, is fleet, and, like the cat,
is a-crawl with curiosity.
Even if a hunter fires a shot,
the guanaco stays to check him out.
To take this beast,
you have to snare its mind.
This thoughtful creature also
gathers its dung in a distinctive ring.

The alpaca, slightly tame,
grazes in the wild,
but at shearing time, will deign
to be herded to villages for clipping.
If you're allotted wool by the alpaca,
the reason is,
the alpaca would be cool.

Never having been domesticated,
the slender, small vicuna

is the Persian cat of camelids.
In its collective *conscious*,
Inca emperors still sleep on
vicuna blankets.
Its scorn—for those who would accept
the ersatz wool of the sheep merino
as the veritable vicuna—
far exceeds its weight.
Now all the camelids give wool
(as do all the sheep),
but there is wool, and then there's wool,
and camelids perceive the sheep as woolless.

The llamas, whether pronounced with *y* or *l*,
are the most familiar.
What's Peru or Ecuador
without another llama? Llama-llama!
The females give both flesh and milk;
male llama meat is tough.
Llama hair is braided into rope;
llama dung is fuel;
llama skins are tanned;
llamas are candle tallow.
If you overload a llama or—
worse—try to ride it,
the llama looks and spits contempt,
lies down, and will not move.
Of all the camelids,
the llama seems to deem itself most human.
Just outside Paracas, Peru at a station,
I saw three haughty reclining llamas
blocking all the pumps
as they waited to be fueled.

If You Would Bell the Cat

Speak softly,
carry no big stick when you speak
to cats.
Be like fog, curiosity, grins.
Carry cream. Flaunt fish. Tip on your toes.
Leave room for being swung.

Still, I prophesy no force of
your iron will suffices
to put a spell on cats.
Cats are familiar with every spell.

Cats have taught Nefertiti,
inserted themselves in Samson's riddle,
leapt from limbs in
Western and African movies
to maul your limbs,
walked invisible by Eve in the Garden of Eden,
sucked out babes' breaths for
the taking as if incubi.
And what would sailors be without cat's-paw?

Cats sing in contradistinction
to merely purring.
Rather, cats opt for *bocca chiusa*.
Cats are always humming.
Cats are always *ritardando*.
Cats came into their own with
Eliot (T. S.),
then Webber
(Jesus Lloyd).

Today, when wild animals run tame
and sparse in Tsavo,
and its lions are as rare
as King Solomon's Mines,

and Ghost and The Darkness
sit moth-eaten-stuffed in Chicago,
the great man-eaters
who stopped railroad and bridge
have been resurrected in movie,
are immortalized.
Cats let you think
they have only nine lives.

Flying Buttermilk Skies

Travel? Grudge match in our household.
Bane of Josh's existence.
Josh? Bane of mine.
Traveling? Tonic for sore souls.
Pardon my assumption:
travel woven into troth we plighted.
Josh would rather suffer lock jaw than make us
members of that "TOURIST CLASS TRASH."
Innocently: "Why can't I just wring your neck,
then encase it in plaster so we can travel?"

I dream covered-wagon-loads of The Old West,
see them trailing dust into the sunset,
begin to embellish my wheedlings
with moonlit riverbanks,
mackerel skies splattered with stars—
Josh, engineer that he is, interrupts:
"I prefer a curvilinear star pattern.
Moreover, mackerel skies have to do
with clouds, not stars."
English teacher that I am,
I'd been more worried about "mackerel skies
splattered with stars" as sin of redundancy.
"You can just stay home and patrol our property
on a lop-eared rocking horse!" was my final say.

As per usual, Josh shot from the hip.
Morning's "mackerel skies" ghost-rode
package on kitchen range.
New Mackinaw with airline tickets, note:
"Muchacha, don't pout like a big old
Mackinaw turtle with his head up his shell.
I'd fly *buttermilk* skies to break trail with you."
I forgave the "Mackinaw turtle" redundancy.

Sea Cat

You perhaps think
cats and water do not mix.
I can assure you,
there have been ship cats
from before the time of ships.

Cats are always beyond the curve.
We have prophetic powers,
but accompanied by
a certain touch of Cassandra.
Men know better than to say
"c—" aboard ship
but do not understand that,
would they simply watch us closely,
they would know
when to jump ship themselves.
Being able to read the future,
we do not remain afloat
when another ship will collide with ours,
a storm will sink our ship,
a torpedo explode it,
or a reef bash it.

If we cats are lively, a storm is brewing.
If the doldrums take you,
place us under a basket on your deck;
you will soon find the wind rising,
conditions changing for the better.

Are you man or mouse?
Take a cat to sea!

Battles of <u>Actium</u>

Once upon a time in the West—
the "Charlton Heston
Name My Autobiography Contest."
I propounded, feeling it not right to
"propose" for Mr. Heston,
Battles of <u>Actium</u>: The Life of Charlton Heston.
I also pontificated: "Mr. Heston has played in
Antony and Cleopatra,
well knows 'Mark Antony's defeat
at Actium changed the course of
history profoundly, [sic] yet Plutarch
covers it thinly,' as he says in
'Arms and the Man' (*Patrick O'Brian*).
Battles of Actium suggests the
epic stature of man and actor,
reminds us of how often we rebound and overcome
(e.g., Moses from the tablets,
Antony from ignominy,
Mr. Heston from typecasting),
and hints at his political stances
("battles" of another kind).
Explaining its allusion in the Preface or wherever,
he can reveal his rich vein of knowledge
(as evidenced in his essay on O'Brian);
surely, letting that side be seen
is important for this contemporary icon.
My title also puns (Actium-acting-actor),
leavening with humor
and reaching for the larger fusion
of Mr. Heston with THEATRE."
The title chosen for Mr. Heston's book
was thoroughly plebeian!
I should have known:
the contest title lacked hyphens!

Christmas Failures

A "Whitman's Sampler" I now give
as 'twas given unto me by Uncle Bob.
I groaned inwardly, annually,
at the dulling of expectation,
at the expectation of expectoration.
You see, my mother made me
eat the awful pieces, too.
I grimace still to think of that
brownish-black-jellied-goop one
that made me, though ever so
Christmas-polite, want to spit.

Seafoam and fudge I now can make
in close approximation of my mother's best.
My children, like me,
came to expect them each Christmas.
My mother also, inadvertently,
taught me not to color seafoam.
We children looked upon her palette
as pretentiously weird.
My father maintained her seafoam
looked like mashed jellyfish.

What I cannot do,
though I have made it a mission,
is find the hard Christmas candy
of my youth. Its lines and forms were distinct;
its colors, too. Its taste—and color—
stuck through the very last suck.
Now, it's all small, flower-shaped,
ribboned, or rounded;
goes to white immediately;
its taste dissipates to bland;
it shatters easily,
leaving nothing for you to best.

Snakes in the Sass

Wild for Black Chicory Coffee

Café au lait is not *pour les hommes*
but is a Creole lady's dish.

Café brûlot? Mais oui!
Brandy and other liqueurs strong,
*stud*ded with cloved orange peel.
The Creoles *peut-être* would say
"infused with strips of
orange peel clove-studded."
But then, alas, Creole custom dictates
coffee brewed in "drip" pot!
Nothing dripped is manly (*hom*me*ly*?)!

Café brûlot diabolique?
Brandy, spices, the whole well-flamed.
Creoles would say *flambé* (*flambée?*).

Café diable? Liqueurs and lemon peel.
C'est bon! Rum and Haitian bitters
and a sturdy, good port
will also see the manly through a storm.

Oh, but give this Cajun *homme*
black chicory coffee!
All the rest are coffee tangents.
My thick Acadian coffee
makes Creoles look limp.
Round it with a *gouté*,
just a taste of sweet: vanilla ice cream
sprinkled with cayenne. Hein! I go wild!
Laissez les bons *coffees* rouler!
Black chicory coffee—*c'est bon! c'est tout!*

Misnomer
(Inspired by *Così fan tutte ossia La scuola degli amanti:
They're All Like That, or The School for Lovers*)

Così fan tutte. "Women All the Same"?
The very title makes me take offence.
This operatic trifle's won acclaim?
It must be for da Ponte's prurience.

I see it in the Sydney Opera House.
The modernized *sur*titles make it worse.
Why couldn't it have been *Die Fledermaus*?
Librettists need the grace to be more terse.

Lights down. And then came Mozart's *Overture* . . . .
The music piqued, depicted, pomped, bemoaned . . . .
"Il core vi dono" leapt from the score.
I was enticed, my every plaint unthroned.

This music climbs above a puerile text.
The School for [Music] Lovers call it next!

La Coiffeuse et La Voyageuse

"Why, I can't believe you didn't know!
Steiner's of London serves
The Queen, Queen Mother, Princess Anne,
and formerly the Lady Di.
Not Camilla Parker-Bowles.
Steiner's is not *vogué* with the horsy set,
always excepting Ascot.

Is this your first time aboard
the *Rotterdam's* World Cruise?
As I am sure you know,
you'll not enjoy *Le Voyage* at all
unless you are coiffured.

Really, we must vamp you up.
The color of your hair is
not the right one for your skin.
And while we're at it, you need fringe.
Oh, dear! Oh, dear! Your scalp is quite,
quite tight. Thinking is not good for women.
It stresses hair *and* scalp!
Please to try this serum.
Three drops a morning dancing on your finger tips.
Just rub it through—but gently!—
and out into the ends.
And I well see that you can use
La Therapie of Paris's 'Masque Pour les Yeux'
and its companion vial,
'La Nourrisante Pour la Peau.'
I just adore the French!
I think that by the end of *Le Tour du Monde*,
we will almost have you coming right.
Of course, you really must let us
peel your skin, massage your thighs
to flatten and to tone them
(the same for cheeks and hips).

We'll de-*cornu* your toes down into
subcutaneous tissue, paint their nails.
Monique will design your personal sets

of fingernails to match your gown
for every Captain's Ball.
We have a special for you, too,
for you Americans, we find,
do so like *Les Spéciàls*.
Every ball-night afternoon,
you may have a free comb-out
and farding if you purchase
our Steiner's weekly package:
Le Marché une Fois par Semaine.
Another item that you need is
'Devil's Mint: The Body Scrub.'
It's by Aromatique, smells
magnifique, splendide!"

Upon exiting Le Salon de Steiner,
I self-rejuvenated sans benefit
of rejuvenation cream,
for in the more plebeian air,
my scalp relaxed and let me think again.
And when I thought, an ion of ironic *logique*
wafted out to the ends of my serum-treated hair:
People simply do not die,
Mon Petit Cabbáge, from ugly hair.

Back Roads Nomenclature

It used to be back roads were lanes,
shortcut walking paths to country worlds
of stills, favorite berry patches,
persimmon trees, ponds, branches
where children played
away from grownups . . . .

That's all changed.
Back roads are named now—
not just "County Road 19"
but names of those who people or
once-peopled them.
"Veach's Mill Road."
"Zeke Anderson's Tavern Lane."
"Mrs. Snookie Perry's Byway."
"Barbecue Hollow Way."
"Old Man Glover's Grove Road."
"Black Bear Branch Swamp Way."

I like that people get their due
in backwoods nomenclature.
Still, I fear.
I fear that desperately smart
young Yankee types
will come sniffing out
our quaint, quaint lives
for documentaries and such,
now that back roads have
risen to nomenclature.

Eschewing The Flat and The Dull

They block off every one of your holes,
set traps in your way.
You build a new-better hole.

One thought or image floats
through your brain.
You take it in your fingers,
mold from it a piece of prose,
piece of poetry,
painting,
something well done,
something kindly done.

You are content to make
little worlds made cunningly.

You take the stuff of your place,
create it into the stuff of your race.

You transform pain into wisdom.

You won't give flat, dull things peace.

You won't give flat, dull people peace.

Of Ashes, Scraps, Scrapes, and Dirty-Word Stories

In the Anchorage airport, my husband looks
for a coat-pocket-sized book.
I pull a eureka,
announce Frank McCourt's *Angela's Ashes*
lately out in paperback.
On a recent cruise, Frank's brother,
actor-writer Malachy
off-color-lectured.
How we loved that droll-sly,
Joyce-toned, great-girthed, rosy-cheeked Irishman.

We're in our motel room in Valdez
(place of disaster by earthquake and oil
but not, I pray, for my upcoming play).
I'm writing at my laptop, am deep, deep in.

From around a corner of our icy polar-bear-
caved room, my husband asks, excitedly,
"Have you ever heard
of . . . 'Cook-u-lain,' as he's certainly not?"
I'm excited, too: "Cuchulain."
I shoot back my scraps: "Ireland's epic hero.
Wielded a giant hockey stick.
From my Old Irish course in grad school.
We read the *Tain-Bo-Cuailgne*,
which is much about him. Why?"
"Do you know how he got his wife?"
"No. Not even who she is or that she was.
I never heard of her."

"Neither had Frankie McCourt.
His buddy Mikey told Malachy and him
Cuchulain wanted to marry.
King Conor MacNessa cautioned:

'Now, Cu, all Irish women want you.
You're bad for Irish men.
A pissing contest we'll have.
Assemble all the Irish women
on Muirthemne's plains.
Whoever does it longest
gets you.' Great Bladdered Emer,
still so-called in Ireland, was the winner,
became Cuchulain's bride.
But Mikey, with the tale,
set Frank up to fail,
for Frank laughed at the *p*-word,
ruining his First Confession.
Had to tell the priest the *p*-word."

The Deck Autumn Deals

Our deck lies quietly dun
against our brown house,
their monochromatics modern and drab.
Our deck, starved for color,
rises a story up,
wraps the house three-quarters,
reaches out and out into the woods.
The world is too cold
on our deck in winter,
too hot in summer,
too rainy in spring.

But in Autumn,
our deck is alive.
With Autumn in the wind,
the paint of our deck stirs,
smelling Autumn coming through the woods,
yet afar-off but coming, coming,
inch by inch, color by color,
wood-smoke smell taking the point.
Our deck and we sniff, breathe long-in,
bears a-rear,
moving our heads in the pregnant air.
Our deck's built-in benches
come to attention;
the round glass-topped deck table
shakes off its own dust,
though we must still
wipe its attendant chairs—
are elated to do so. We share our
deck's enbrisking as Autumn approaches.

And then one morning, deck and all,
we awaken from our beds
to the shock of Autumn's palette,

somehow unprepared for
Nature's natural psychedelics.

For the brief whole of Autumn,
we eat on our deck when we can
or watch Autumn dance through
the pulsing glass of window and door.

And then one morning, deck and all,
we awaken from our beds
to the shock of Autumn's casket.
The first leaf has scarcely settled
on our deck's floor
when the rain of leaves storms.
The reign of Autumn is over.
Forgetful, enjoying rustle, cracking,
we sweep the curled and knotted brown leaves
off the precipice of our deck and
pronounce the benediction,
"The last of the Mohicans," nodding wisely.
Then we old bears
and the Deck Bear, too,
sleep once more,
dreaming of the coming Autumn,
which always has an ace up its leaves.

The Dogma of Poetry

My husband used
not to like poetry readings,
even when his wife was reading.
Then I won an award or two in
The Fifteenth Annual . . . ,
and he went.
That was the day he took
the dogleg toward poetry.
A psychologist, he says
partial reinforcement's a real bitch.

A mother was there to read
"Gone But Not Forgotten"
for her son,
who had won "Honorable Mention"
in the "Student Category."
"Gone But Not Forgotten" was a canine
but was not for K-9—
the son was away at college.

By the time all this was explained,
my husband was alerted
that the untoward was toward us,
and he was here as star-crossed,
not just a dog at heel lest
he be exiled in the doghouse.

So were we both. Both
star-crossed that day at the
Poetry Reading Awards Contest
of The Fifteenth Annual . . . .

The star of the day was the
dog in absentia,
pet of the poet in absentia.
When their time came, the mother,

in the failure of both stars to rise,
rose to say: "I can't do this.
I'll cry."
And she did.
Right there in front of her chair.
She never made it to the stage.

One of those ladies who
hang out in poetry readings
bounded into the breach, baying:
"I'll read for you! Oh,
please let me read for you!
It would be my great pleasure."
And so she did. Or tried to.
By the time, about the second line,
the dead dog had been buried
in his master's Vietnam
flight jacket in the back yard,
her torrent of words
became a torrent of tears.
Not crocodile tears either.

I'm too busy ferreting out
how the poet can qualify for
the "Student Category"
and still be a Vietnam veteran
and Mr. Joe College.

My husband nudges me:
"Remember that song
'It's Crying Time Again'?
Well, it's back—and barking!
But people always cry for the 'underdog'.
Did he give the dog his dog tags,
do you think?
Hey, for once,
I encourage you to use your
dog-ear trick!"

Not to be outdone, I retort:
"Remember Alice's tears almost
drowning the White Rabbit?
Wonder what Lewis Carol
had against dogs?"

We never did hear
the rest of that poem,
but we think of it often.
On trips, not just to Dogger Banks
or by dogcart or dogger,
as if it were one of those competitive haiku,
we make up lines for that poem,
seek a name for That Dog.
And both of us cheat.
Of that I am certain.
Cheat and pun. Pun and cheat.
And tongue in cheek.
In more ways than one.

"The dog's name was Sirius," he says.
"Get serious," I say,
my canines dropping
saliva for my sharpness.

"The owner," he says, "had a
Canis Major.
He got it in Obedience School."
"Well, I'll be doggoned.
Where did you fetch that one from?
Maybe that explains how the poet qualified
for 'Student Category.'"

Both fans of Patrick O'Brian,
we now dog each other
with such bones
as eating "dog's body" and
drinking "dog's nose"
(and hair of the dog),

Snakes in the Sass

a bad case of dog-eat-dog
but better than dogfish.
It's become a regular dogfight.

He has a dog-vane on his
weather gunwale,
and we're always on the dog-watch
with our dog paddles
made of dogwood.
"Now who's dogmatic?" I ask.

"Gone But Never Forgotten"
has lighted up
our poetry life.

"Why is a dogie a calf? . . .
Because he's not a 'doggy'—d-o-g-*g-y*!"

"The Dog Star is only 8.6
light-years from earth."
"You're straining at the leash for that one. . . .

It's also called 'Sothis.'"
"*So this* is the Dog Star?"
We ask it together.

"Well, he was for sure the star
of that poetry reading!"
I say doggedly.
"It was a case of the dog
being the catcher."

I can't swear my husband
loves poetry,
but he'll go to the dogs
for doggerel.
My husband definitely
digs doggerel!

Dry Bones Rise *Driza-Bone* Again

Today I bought my husband
what reputes to have longevity
to last unto family heirloom—
his reward for climbing Sydney Harbor Bridge.
I bought said husband one Driza-Bone dilly bag.

Then give your sweet love a token,
for he is safely down
from the high and windy bridge!
Oh, give your love a token
that he'll go no more a-climbing
that high and windy bridge!

Australian greatcoats, dilly bags, sou'westers,
slouch hats, and such come long-lineaged,
make sailors' knots of desert and sea.
Another canny, frugal Scotsman (*Le* Roy, not *Rob*)
made oilskin rainwear for sailing ships
from *used* lightweight sails, waterproofed the cotton
with linseed oil, didn't think of tar.

With hey-ho a down dilly
for the canny, frugal Scotsman!
He thought of tars but didn't,
though they went upon the sea!

Aussie "squatters" learned
this sailwear from sailor lore,
plied pressganging of their own—
demanded longer coat for horseback,
fantail a-stern to shelter saddle;
leg straps to belay the flapping;
wrist straps to stay arms from hoaring—
h-o-a-r-i-n-g as from the cold . . . .
Mêlées resulted when sailcloth landlubbered.

Oh, pipe, Men, pipe!
And let the ship wear!
Pipe to get our boys home!
Back to the sea and Botany Bay!

In Australia's long, hot summers,
the linseed oil dried, was petrified, went cracked.

Wail-away, wail-away,
the cloth so hard,
the Wait-a-Bit had to wait a bit to catch
while the cracks let in the rain!

Then "Driza-Bone" was born
of Le Roy out of T. E. Pearson's Sandsoap.
"Driza-Bone"? Why, Aussie "dry as a bone"—
like animal skulls and crossbones in Australia's arid land.

Oh, Jubilee! Oh, Jubilant!
Driza-Bone links desert-sea
in that Great, Great Land Down Under
when my man turns home again
from that high and windy bridge!

Apologia for The Dozens

We complain when
Black kids do The Dozens.
At "your mother this,"
"your mother that,"
most turn up their noses,
deem the perpetrators plain uncouth.

But what we must consider is the lineage.
Go to the Greeks for stichomythia.
Go to dialoging Pastoral shepherds.
(The capital prevents redundancy.)
Verbal dueling.
The sweetest mutual abuse.
Go to Shakespeare, Pet.
Elizabeth and Richard,
Anne and Gloucester in *Richard III*;
Hero and Don Pedro in *Much Ado*
(which is what we are about The Dozens);
Hermia-Lysander in
A Midsummer Night's Dream
(ditto for what we are about The Dozens).
Even women do it!
It's all about nuances of the voice.

And that slapping palms,
pointing fingers?
Shakespeare's—and Italians'—figs!

Eagle on a Hot Tin Roof

Fresh from Ogalala Scout Camp,
the four freshmen suffer through Freshman Orientation,
steal a night off to frolic, see their first movie
in the Big City.
Could even a Boy Scout resist
a sixteen-foot-long picture of Elizabeth Taylor
in sheer slip
reclining atop the movie marquee
as Maggie the Cat in the South's own
Cat On a Hot Tin Roof
(though this is not Tennessee)?

The movie's out about eleven.
That reclining Liz, glued to *sheet* rock
("How appropriate!" they think.)
and in a wooden frame,
has toyed with them throughout,
a virtual cat playing with these boy mice.
They ponder;
puzzle what to do;
more than one pontificates.

They hoist their smallest member atop the theater.
He kicks Miss Taylor loose,
though hesitant thus to approach her,
passes her down, solemnly, gingerly.
They place all sixteen feet of her on top of their car,
holding that precious cargo
through the rolled-down windows.
Surely, Miss Taylor makes the car go faster,
gives that old hand-me-down-car Paradise wings!
They drive down Main Street, Big City
(though this is not the Nile, that car no barge).

The room of the Idea Boy is only fourteen feet wide.
Two feet of Miss Taylor (and her own two feet)
must recline in the closet
(the start, perhaps, of her line of scent?).
At night, when the room is lighted,
Liz is a Bat Man signal silhouetted on the shade.
Liz is in the line of sight.

In a few days, the police answer the signal,
take names.
The theater manager would drop the charges;
the police won't.
The boys' lawyer must choose one among them
to take the seat to the judge's left,
where no moss grows.
That seat will be hot like tin blistered by the sun,
but the Scouts, for the first time
since encountering Miss Taylor,
are oblivious.
The one the lawyer chooses is an Eagle Scout,
who also sang in the church choir,
must solo here.

"Son, why did you do it?"
The judge tries to be stern,
realizes he should have omitted the "Son,"
but the Eagle Scout, twitching on his tin,
is oblivious.
"I thought it would . . . look-nice-in-our-room!"
The courtroom corrupts into laughter.
The judge tries to be stern,
but the lawyer, if not the Scouts,
sees him eyeing the reclining Miss Taylor.
That winsome lady may even wink.

"Because you're an Eagle Scout,
I choose to believe this escapade
a schoolboy prank."
The judge's *schoolboy* will later smart

(but in more ways than one).
For now, paying to have Miss Taylor
repositioned seems a small price.
The Eagle soars again.

Why Johnny Can't Equatorialize

Were the cartographers crazy?
Zero degrees, zero minutes, zero seconds?
What a line!
Greenwich grinned: it got the zero point.
What latitude!
(The widest latitude line ringing the earth.)

The equator—midway between the poles.
A terrestrial great circle,
its plane perpendicular to the polar axis.
Imaginary line around our globe
to give us hemispheres.

Easing through exotic places:
Brazil, Colombia, the Galapagos;
Indonesia; Somalia, Kenya, Uganda, Zaire.
The turning point for our seasons,
reversed for our hemispheres.
Center point of our earth and of the tropics,
that area between Cancer and Capricorn.
Or is that getting Zodiacal?

The equator has no rain forest;
we can let down our environmental guard.
Equator Longitudinal—the Prime Meridian.
Equator Magnetic.
Oh, it draws us to it!

And then there's the Equator Comical:
calling all pollywogs,
those Equator-Crossing Tyros,
who must libate to King Neptune
and kiss his royal fish.
Oh what latitude doth man thus give himself
to make of a sea tale a world-and-fish-scale!
For when King Neptune in his horse-drawn chariot,

his horses with golden manes and brazen hoofs,
skims in his chariot across the sea,
the sea smoothes itself before him.
All mankind must pay homage to Neptune
to gain smooth waters and passage safe.

Kiss a frog and get a prince.
Kiss a pollywog—get the equator.
Passion, they say, is hot.

EVA [Extra-Vehicular Activity]

EVA was eventful, though Mother would have fied upon those big, clumsy feet come out her, dismissed her as just another *lunar*tic (like me).

EVA could tongue-tangle, too. Her *man, men,* and *mankind* were not to my liking. She slighted all articles, definite and indefinite alike. I, with all the other wooers, tongue-tangled, too. *Chaste* lost out in our translation. We *chased* the moon through EVA. Apollo was her brother, not her lover.

Her stepping and leaping, literal and figurative, kept all suitors hopping and hoping. She was always scrubbing and probing. I knew the moon dust she showered was not just for me. I knew her solar winds could desiccate me.

But EVA was extract of extra, a lunar beignet who filled in each hole of all the green cheese. She had a mission. It was Mr. Poe's *In Sunshine and Shadow* that enticed our EVA, not NASA's Honeysuckle Creek or Down Under's Parkes.

I was late. Other knights on other nights—Aldrin, Armstrong—cast shadows upon my heart. Though I have ridden boldly over the Mountains of the Moon, I stay in the Valley of the Shadow. Still, I've found my Eldorado if only in mind's shadows. I am Keeper of the Shadow, showing seekers—EVA is Eldorado! They also serve who only stand and tell: EVA, flight before her, came in peace for all mankind. Her message I ungarble.

When Flowers Play at Telephone
[A Parody of Frost and "The Telephone"]

Rob
"Never have I traversed such a distance from Elinor
since we were married.
Somewhat tired, I think I shall sit,
though so anxious to be home.
What a pleasant place!
Robert Herrick doubtless
visited many such places
to fill his flower poems.
But, truth to say, I would prefer
companionship. Elinor's.
Even so, alone here as I am,
I wish the flowers could talk . . . .
Thinks Elinor of me?
And if she so thinks, what thinks she?
Hark? What is this I hear? . . .
Ah, a buzz.
Bees, at least, if not flowers, talk,
after their fashion."

Elinor
"All those vows of eternal closeness,
vows antedating the formal marriage,
and now this loving couple is apart.
Where has he wandered, this star-struck,
flower-fascinated swain of mine?
Yet I would not appear over-anxious,
break from the persona I have created.
Thus do we trap ourselves
in webs of our own conceiving.
Or would Rob say *de*ceiving?
My heart calls, 'Come! Return!'
No! My mind cautions my tongue to hold.
No, I *must* not.

I would not, by the slightest action,
yield to the urge to turn pursuer,
eschew the role of the pursued.
About my household tasks, then,
as if indifferent.
Thus will he find me when he,
at length, home returns."

Rob
"No bee that is, but sympathy total
'twixt Nature and this poor errant husband.
And yet, I know the fool
others would say I am,
dared I admit to think
the very flowers played at telephone
to link two lovers.
Still, if some lover such as I
were at-watch, hidden here,
he would see, I swear—
and not only see but *hear*—
this or-else *fancied* connection between two souls.
The flower plays telephone, rings!
To pretend this sound not real is Love—
and Nature—to disdain.
Then I the fool will play,
will cease with denial coy and respond!
Let me, then, take up the receiver
of this same flower-telephone.
Oh, yes, I hear. She says, 'Come! Return!'
And home I speed, though fearing—knowing—
once there, were I to say to Sweet Elinor,
'I thought I heard you call to me
through a telephone of flowers . . . .'"

Elinor
"Now, Rob, the *idea* I like.
Did I speak,
on this flower-telephone,
poetically?"

Rob
"You said, 'Come! Return!'
And so I did.
Thence here I am."

Elinor
"Use my unsaid words, Sweet Rob,
in a poem.
Audiences are most forgiving."

Feathers in Fortaleza's Cap

Guide Regis delights in his discourse
on City of Sun and Light.
Not the usual tourist fare.

Cashewed and lobstered Fortaleza
has its own tree of life, Great Carnauba,
whose every part is used.
Cattled Fortaleza, non-sugarcaned,
speaks [politically-incorrect] Portuguese,
makes Portuguese butt of jokes:
Portuguese don't drink cold milk because
they can't get cow in freezer;
Portuguese grow big mustaches
to look like their mothers.
Fortaleza's famous writer,
priest José de Allencar,
celebrated Workers' Day
as a ruse to honor birth of
his son by his cousin.

Still, we are not to think badly
of writers [or priests?].
They led first protests against slavery;
his state was first in South America
to free its slaves.
[Today, graffiti writing is rampant.]

A bus sign warns not to smoke
"cigars, pipes, straw cigars."
My confusion over
Cigarro de Palma must be legion,
but Regis merely finds me strange.
"No problema, Senora."

Fortaleza boasts beautiful
Fortress Schoonenbeck, its stones

from Scotland as Portuguese ballast.
Fortaleza has baobab of *Little Prince*,
which elephants eat [were they here].
Fortaleza has "women market"
where women used to show off clothes,
now sell more personal wares.
Fortaleza has ten girls to one man.
["No problema, *Senor!*"]

Gordian Knot Redivivus

Ushuaia, Tierra del Fuego, Argentina,
city southern-most in the world
(Puerto Williams on Navarino Island being village),
needed something more,
our Government was sure,
to grow and prosper.
Our Government decide to cut
Mr. Gordian Knot.

Eureka! Beavers from The Great Canada!
Alas, their fur in Ushuaia
did not grow into the prime,
and the Mister Beavers ate up
all our wood
and made our waters messy.
Spanish rabbits sailed here next
at invitation of our Government.
Their fur was likewise a disaster, and
they ate the grass from under
the feet of our Ushuaian sheep.
We introduced the fox—a grey one—
to take care of Mr. Rabbit.
That sly old fox just ate our lambs.
And now we gots the red fox also,
which is hard to understand.
But our Government grew smarter, too.
Hey, presto, it unleashed a rabbit virus.
After five years, though,
the rabbits have rebounded.
Our leaders say, "Eat rabbits plates,
using skins for souvenir."
We imported Mr. Muskrat
for his perfume.
Something's gone wrong with him,
so—no perfume,

but the tourists still believe
we in Ushuaia smelling good,
and we gots lots of sawmills,
with vegetables and fruits brought in,
petrol but no refineries.
We earning more money
than the rest of our country,
but needing more money
to survive.

The Government learned
Mr. Gordian Knot living already
in Ushuaia.
You see, thanks God, peoples likes to come
to The Last Frontier,
to where we had a penal colony
on our Staten Island,
to The End of the World.
Us Ushuaians calling ourselves "The End."
Thanks God, many peoples
deciding to live forever
in Ushuaia or at least
to do shoppings here
and visit again
in the next future.

Galahading and Galateaing

I love new words
(not of the ilk of *alot*,
quality as adjective).

I love plentiful,
preposterously pompous puns;
food that's good—and pretty;
finding some weird fact;
movie lore galore;
movies Galahadan, Galatean;
traveling 'round the world
being surprised, pleasantly;
loving and being loved;
learning, learning, learning.
I love people (hate meetings).
I love Galahading, Galateaing.
I love *gee's* (not so big on *haw's*).
I love *ess's*, not hisses;
my punster-husband (not just for puns).
Oh, I love to dance (would love to sing),
love to make up words!

Milton is my specialty,
but I also love John Donne.
I love it that, when we're done,
we just go on and on
Galahading, Galateaing.

Hunter-Gatherer

I said it once too often
(though never beating upon my chest):
"I am the Hunter-Gatherer
for this household.
Behold! I have saved
more than I spent this week
by loving attention to
sales and coupon clippings,
the 'buy-one,-get-one-free's,'
the buy-one,-get *two* free's'.
I am The Wily Grocery Shopper!"

My psychologist husband had had enough.
"'Buy-one,-get *two* free's?'
You made that up, surely!
My wife The Great Exaggerator."
(He is not always Psychologist The Wise.)

"Let's see *you* save more than you spend!
I double-coupon-dare you!"
(Psychologists cannot resist a dare;
they are that normal at least.
Mine didn't.)

Off he went, armed with
the Wednesday specials in the local paper.
I warned him (*Splenda*ly) to take
his cell phone to rearrange his schedule.

He was back in under six hours,
head bloody but egoed,
his savings seven cents more than his bill.
His major foe?
Two ladies he'd fought—tongue *and* cheek—
for the last "two-for-the-price-of-one" blueberries,
his favorite. Why, the man had

Snakes in the Sass

followed the spoor
of every antioxidant on sale!
"Are you phobic?" I asked.
"Just radical
about free radicals," he said,
"with an inordinate capacity for antioxidants."
"No rust on you!" I said.

He set, as I supposed, each proud trophy
upon the kitchen counter,
narrating its salvation in savings
to the last precise penny.

I didn't point out that,
even *not* on sale,
house brands would have been less
than the name-brand stars
crowning his plunder.
I've lived among psychologists
long enough to know
when not to eat thunder.

At the end of my husband's show-and-tell,
I kissed him (tongue *in* cheek),
saluted him as a fellow Hunter-Gatherer
in our [grocery-store] cave.
Not once did I fear displacement,
though partial reinforcement's
a roguish bear.
A wise wife knows the art of tongue in *check*,
knows how soon her husband's sated.

Three days beyond The Great Hunt,
I wrestled my way
into the pantry's clutter
(psychological and otherwise)
and found—six boxes of
a new variety of Great Grains cereal:
Maple Pecan Crunch.

When I innocently asked
if he'd hidden it because it wasn't on sale,
he repressed the question, pointing out
that Maple Pecan Crunch
is high in folic acid.
"Maybe its multi-grain flakes
baked with a touch of real maple syrup,"
I slurped, "but *praline pecans*?
You'd better stick to
scavenging free radicals
and let me wage the trophy life,
else you'll be eating *words*!"

Tale in Old Icelandics

One Frederick Tudor of Nahant
looked at his pond and saw his chance.
He'd get Southerners to buy his ice.

"Crazy Tudor" others thought him.
If the "fish peddler" is a vessel
sans a mighty catch,

what to call the schooner
with a lade that melts?
Like all who have succeeded,

Tudor pshawed condemning words,
prayed for blizzards, white-outs, and the like,
would have turned his very soul to ice.

Frederick Tudor of Nahant set his ice-blue eyes
on Charleston before the War of 1812.
How those grandees loved that ice!

Even as the blizzards howled,
Mr. Tudor cut ice blocks in winter,
filled his icehouse 'gainst the spring,

when he loaded down his schooners
with ice in sawdust or the cheaper hay.
Tudor grew annually two crops of ice,

even when the blizzards failed,
deadheaded apples in his ice,
still took time to tutor in Old Icelandics.

From its start at Tudor's Wharf
in bean- and cod-clad Boston,
New England ice

schoonered to West Indies,
rounded Horn to India.
Whereupon I pause to wonder—

it's not ice-crystal-clear to me—
why doesn't the British Empire
like its liquor on the rocks?

Jour Maigre

Every Fish Day was a "lean day"?
Enough to turn me into a fish-wife.
I'd have unleashed my invective,
carped up a flood, except that my daughter
would have looked at me
with those "can-this-be-
my-dear-sweet mother?" big eyes.

My sons got to do Fish Days
with their dad. Meaning,
at least twice a month,
Saturday became an all-day fishing outing
at a semi-local lake. *For them.*

I'm not knocking bonding, you understand.
But, even if I detested fishing,
our daughter Millie might well like it,
and, besides,
 why couldn't the whole family *bond*?
I pictured Husband and Sons
beating their chests
à la Robert Bly over some
panting-its-last-breath bream.
(Do fish pant?)
Tom would remind me that it's a man-thing—
Hemingway . . . Zane Grey.
I baited him with
Patrick O'Brian's Aubrey and Maturin.
(Well, they're always at sea,
even if they don't fish!)

I decided I needed better bait.
Millie and I went *on*-line for our fish.
By the time "our boys" were back from
their bonding, we were no longer *floundering*,

Snakes in the Sass

asserted that we were not *bottom-feeders*,
that we wanted to re-do
the roof in *fishscale* tiles,
were planning to purchase a pitcher plant
to await the appearance of its *fishtail nectary*,
would dress in twin mermaid outfits
each Halloween and let the men of the family
carry us from house to house—
"Well, we couldn't possibly walk
on our fish tails to trick-or-treat,
now could we?" After some thirty minutes of
our mouth-fishing, our fishermen conceded
we were a "pretty kettle of fish
even if we were fish out of water."

We've been bonding *as a family*
for some time now.

All Dogs, Cats, and Fat-Cat Tourists Welcome in China: *Low*ku

Building boom proclaimed.
The scaffolding? All bamboo.
Who's bamboozling whom?

Sweet potatoes roast
on a barrel-rigged brazier.
"Take tourists to shop!"

Lazy Susan whirls,
chop sticks collide in food space,
Westerners red-faced.

Three mattresses move
by girl-pedaled bicycle.
"Take tourists to shop!"

A wild-eyed dog flies
along blood-Red Chinese streets
chasing its scant Life.

Two Chinese children
wash white fluffy dog—oh, why?—
in pink plastic pan.

Red, hot crowds at march.
You can't get out of the way.
You lose pace—and face.

Chinese exercise in parks.
Westerners line dance.
"Take tourists to shop!"

"Time out for me, please,
for Xanadu, Kubla Khan!"
"Take tourists to shop!"

"Yellow Peril" it was.
"Red Menace" it may remain.
Now it's Tourist Trap.

Aristophanic Madang, Papua New Guinea

The Cruise Director comes on the intercom
pleased to describe the [obligatory] "Folkloric Show"
in Madang, Papua New Guinea:
school children will come aboard to sing.
Cute but ho-hum. Children are always nice.
No passenger really listening.
Comes afternoon.
Comes urgent announcement
some fifteen minutes before the show.
The Cruise Director's voice, for once,
moves from its smooth, soothing groove.
"Urgent. Urgent.
Your attention, please. Correction. Correction.
The Papua New Guinea performers are definitely
not school children.
Please, if you are at all given to squeamishness,
do not attend.
Repeat—DO NOT ATTEND!"
The rest of the message is lost
among the banging doors,
hurrying feet, excited calls.
"Must be topless!"
"I hope so!"
This last from the men.
For the first time, the "Folkloric Show" is SRO.
We look around expectantly at one another,
giggle, wonder.

The drummers take their places,
sit cross-legged across the stage's front.
They're fine. Native costume.
Topless but men.
The actors run on. Ladies first.
One or two middle-aged, non-nubile,
are topless.

Disappointment reigns. But not for long.
The men enter.
A noise swells in the audience,
gist hard to assess.
Then SILENCE.
Awe, perhaps.
The men wear huge phallic sheaths,
shells at tips,
all jiggle-jangling as they dance.
Shades of Aristophanes!
The dancers seem oblivious,
except for one teenager
who flaunts his accouterment,
bounces it up and down,
whirls like a dervish.
Only one lady flees the Queen's Lounge.

After Madang,
neither Holland America
nor its passengers
take the acquisition of culture for granted.
(I think the people of Madang
had great fun with us.)

Mahla of Mumbai in Eden

Best year of my life—I am Mahla of Mumbai—
Mumbai "Bombay" to British—
best year of my life as junior in high school
in Eden, North Carolina, on Rotary scholarship.

Every seventh person in world Indian,
but not in Eden. How to explain to Americans . . . ?
Hundred-ten ways to wear sari. I to teach every one?
Each Indian state having different way.

We having confusion of cockroaches.
In India, cockroaches be
conveyances of three wheels.

In India, no dates. (American friends having dismay.)
Girls and boys slipping out to meet
in Hanging Gardens. Americans thinking,
if caught, being hanged!
Our marriages arranged; are not needing to date.
Much confusion from marry in red.
Red for auspicious.

Disbelief of unshod lady Jains
walking everywhere, never cutting hair but
pulling it from roots, never bathing
but never smelling badly, always wearing white.

Upset of India's swastika-like symbol
for four stages life: bachelorhood, marriage,
journey to death, detachment/courtship of God.
India only country where Jews not persecuted!

Center ultimate wisdom between brows.
Friends making faces. Indian men doing
no domestic work. Marigold being sacred.

Two girls or boys holding hands mean friendship.
Worshipping at Sufi mosques on months of five Fridays
making wish to come true. Tikkas or bhindis
not caste marks but for the good luck.
Am thinking I taught them stick-on tattoos.

Americans accept cow sacred
but laugh at sacred cow.
They try, try, try to get Mahla
to eat hamburger. I could not.
I must to my country be true.

I flew home via Canada.
In airport in Canada, I slip in McDonald's,
eat Big Mac. Most delicious.
No American friends seeing.
I saying to myself, I was Eve.
Old serpent of Eden eating me.

Mickey Mousing

Once upon a cheese,
I was holed
before The Great Mouse King.
"Your mission is to raise our status
among mankind. To end this fatuous pitting
of man against mouse,
for the human race
begins thus to efface itself."
Whereupon, The Great Mouse King
misted me
with magic essence of Edam,
and I was up and off.

I awoke in Mr. Disney's studio
with ears like blowing black ping pong bats
and boots bigger than the feet of
The Great Mouse King.
The man who claimed
to animate me was "Ub Iwerks,"
which seemed to me
great Great Mouse King wit.

Fortunately, Mrs. Disney named me;
as "Mickey" I debuted.
But in my first two shorts,
no one spoke.
We effected at most
some mousy little jokes.

Now it seemed to me,
to meet my mission,
I couldn't be as silent as mice by custom,
humans being *hearing* creatures
and we mice having learned
to bell the cat.

I called upon The Great Mouse King,
who'd recently insinuated sound
into the feature film.
And The Great Mouse King
baited Mr. Disney's trap,
and, Presto-Cheeso,
Dear Walt felt this urge
to invest us all
with voices and speak them all himself.

And The Great Mouse King, further,
led Mr. Disney to install
Mr. Stalling's music
and synchronize our images
and voices to its notes.
This was 1928, as your years go,
in *Steamboat Willie*,
the first animated cartoon
with voices and music.

I was most pleased that Mr. Disney
did not make me squeak or go about
(all praise to The Great Mouse King!)
on little cat feet.

And from that time,
man has called synchronizing
images and music "Mickey Mousing,"
and all mankind has been kind
to this poor mouse,
who is not without honor
in The Land of Mice.

Of Lombok's Land-Bound Monkeys, Short-Tailed Cats

Far, far back (when the world
was still sorting itself out
for the Next-Near-Future),
in Lombok, Indonesia,
The Monkey and The Cat
competed in a game of chess.
Mr. Cat won, whereupon Mr. Monkey,
miffed, bit off his tail.
To this day, the cats
in Lombok, Indonesia, have short tails.

But, in Lombok, Indonesia,
cats are sacred; monkeys aren't.
Even now, to harm a cat
calls down most dreadful luck.
Killing a cat—well,
the most to be hoped for,
after you have sacrificed to give
Mr. Cat the highest proper burial,
is that his vengeance will not spread
father to son, mother to daughter,
generation unto generation.

But what did Mr. Cat do to Mr. Monkey?
Oh, Mr. Cat was clever.
He made the monkeys sit still
upon the up side of
Lombok's great mountain.
(which is precisely why
you never see any monkeys
on the down side where
they can frolic freely in the trees).

Today, when you drive up Baun Pusuk,
the road laid out by the Japanese
in World War II,
you will see the monkeys as they
sit upon the guardrail and its posts
to watch you pass.
Not a one will take to tree
or cut accustomed monkey shines.
They will sit quite still and peer,
hoping you have influence with Mr. Cat.

When you reach the mountain top
and climb up to view the shrine
and all the short-tailed cats therein,
you will walk past the monkeys massed below.
If you observe them closely,
you will see a tuft of hair
on their heads between their ears—
the residua of cat tail.
And if you listen very carefully,
you may hear the wisest of them
sigh and say, "Oh, never—I, The Monkey,
beg you—never cross The Cat!"

Leporidae in the Grass

On our way to Valdez's Totem Inn
for dinner, my husband points.
Two beagle-sized rabbits,
piebald like Tonto's Scout,
cute and clever, leapfrog along
the restaurant's flower bed.
The one in front nibbles,
then stands guard for the other.
They slip under cars when noise threatens.
We follow along,
watching them select tender green shoots,
eschew blossoms, chat to each other.
The same plump size.
Bucks out to start the weekend
with a fling in someone else's warren?

Mighty hunters lurk? What's afoot
in The Land of the Last Frontier,
place of salmon, halibut, seals, whales,
bears of four kinds, superior eagles,
fussing-strutting-puffed-up crows,
many-splendored creatures?

As the restaurant door opens,
we move to block Whoever's view
of the careless rabbits
munching along, unmindful of our service,
obviously ignorant of Mr. MacGregor.

Mechanical to fetch foolish tourists in?
"Snake(s) in the grass" writ large?

Pique of the Moon

That Armstrong and Aldrin—
Twiddledum and Twiddledumber—
claimed the descent engine
"left no crater of any size."
That the one where the probe first hit
was merely a "minus-Y."
Right, and any *decent* engine
would roll right over them for expecting
a Ms. Mousy Moon to begin with.
They accused me of having vesicles
in my surface, of suffering from "phenocrysts."
They did admit my "stark beauty"
but linked it to the high desert of the USA.
I'm unique! Can't Americans find
a measure beyond themselves!
The best they could come up with?
Magnificent desolation.
Magnificent, yes, but *desolation*?
Another case of mankind going
one step too far. And then they had to
jab that plaque on my peak. That plaque
did nothing for my peak *or* pique.
But I have landed one, too.
Once they took that first small step,
those earthlings had to come up with
something new under the *Moon*.
No longer could they say,
"You act as if we're asking for the Moon."
No longer could they believe
moonshine's just for drinking!

Feet Smart(s) in Granada, Nicaragua

We have an hour in the central square
where folkdancers entertain,
vendors besiege,
bicycles buzz us,
and horse-drawn carriages want us.
I mistake a hammock "spreader" for
the Nicaraguan version of the diggeridoo.

All the park benches have missing slats,
as if not to detain too long.
When I sit on one,
a shoe-shine boy,
probably nine, is instantly before me
cutting me off at the pass
with his three-legged stool.
I say no, pleasantly but firmly.
Who polishes black tennis shoes?
He should offer to wipe off
the accumulated salt (then sell it).
But he's street-wise, too,
flirts, winks, faux-moues,
puts Miss Bette Davis's eyes
out to Elsie the Cow's pasture,
is well on his way to "hunk."
AND KNOWS IT.
Still, I relent.

The only English he deigns to know
is "Chang!" It must be shouted harshly
several times before I learn
to exchange my feet.

My husband, the one who's smiled
with such superiority,
gives him an extra dollar

and takes digital pictures
of the "Shoe-Shine Scene,"
with a close-up of one shining shoe
to "commemorate" his wife's succumbing.

Oh, Say, Can You *Sing* ... ?

Make a presentation at the
First Annual Convention of the
National [Asian] Indian American
Chamber of Commerce?
At the Willard Hotel
in Washington, D.C.?
I'd be delighted!
An hour before I leave for the airport,
the call from the conference dignitary:
"Pleasing to say,
Dr.-Madam listed on banquet program
to lead 'Star Spangled Banner,'
have honorable place
at high banquet table."
If I don't sing,
I also don't argue with Raj English.
I'm thinking . . . .
Jump in the car; head for the local library;
check out a book on national anthems;
sit down at the computer;
prepare a "performance" poem
of "The Star-spangled Banner"
replete with historical notes.
Hang out the banner!
Hang the stars!
I'm home-on-the-range!

Comes the banquet—
with me
the only woman and non-Indian
at the head table.

Comes and comes the banquet:
Indian dignitaries,
Senators, everything

but the devoutly-to-be-wished-for
parade of pachyderms.
At length, the major domo
is wending his way toward me.
I straighten.
"Sorry to say, please,
necessity for speakers to meet
schedules, etc., etc.,
United States of American anthem delayed."
Comes and comes the delay.

Nearly midnight.
The major domo is wending his way
toward me:
"Please to apologize.
Due to lateness of hour, please,
having no United States of American anthem."

Indians, please, too polite to notice, please,
when I leapt into the air,
clicked my heels together,
and wended my way
out of the Willard's banquet hall.

The Secret Life of Trains

Your parents give you a little wooden train.
You're bored because it's so "wooden."
You try to make it squall around curves,
blow its whistle, ring its bells.
You're bored.
When it's your turn to
take the rite of pass*enger*—
to change from wooden to electric—
on that fated Christmas morning,
what to your wondering eyes should appear?

What you think about what is under that tree
is a secret you keep from your parents.
You are poised to embark on your sea of trains;
the train isn't from the right side of the tracks.
Electric but *red* and, worse, red *plastic*,
it doesn't look like a train.
Nothing else in the
wide world whole
looks exactly like a train!

Before you reach the tree that morning,
you have said good-bye to Toyland.
You did not like cheap toys then;
you do not like cheap toys now;
you will not like cheap toys
when you play with the electric chain saws
and model trains of your adulthood.

But what do you say to your parents?
"Oh, that train, that train, how can I *express*
what I feel on this Christmas full of wonders!"

Not that you mean to tell your parents a fib.
It's just that the track isn't always clear.

You can't always say exactly what you feel.
Parents get their feelings hurt pretty quick,
get disappointed same as you.
They don't always not know better;
maybe they can't *afford* better.

To try to make a "special" out of a "local,"
you begin your daily ritual of waving
from your front step in the imaginary direction
of your imaginary friends
on the imaginary train
that passes every unimaginary morning
as you leave for school.
Your parents say,
"Weren't we wise to buy our child that train?
It doesn't take an Einstein to make the connection
between children and trains, you know."

Sheepish Over Ewe: Comeuppance to Apathy

Who cares if New Zealand has
fifteen sheep per person!
The Land of the Long White Cloud is
named for sheep fleece?
What bull!
Those Kiwis like to clown around!

I want to see the Glow Worm Grotto!
Hear Milford Sound!
Feed me a Hangi meal!
I've been practicing that
Maori challenge with the tongue!

I'd rather smell Rotoruan sul*phur*
than sheep dip!
I've seen sheep, counted them!
They weren't so hot in *Babe*.

Agrodome?
That can't be the spelling!
Nineteen meat and wool breeds posed
upon tiered stage?
Who would—?

Look at that big Drysdale!
He's a Romney with a special gene
giving medullated fibers.
("Non-crimpy" to those out of the loop.)

Lanolin? That's wool fat
for lipsticks, skin creams.

Captain Cook brought sheep here, you know.
The main breed is the Romney,
named for England's Romney Marsh.

Best overall carpet wool.

The Kiwis are the largest producers
of crossbred (strong!) wool.
(China's but a distant second.)
Merino, Cheviot, Coopworth, Perendale,
Lincoln, Border Leicester—
I won't bore you with all nineteen.
Or those of Araparva Island.

The Shearer is a *Compere*;
the sheep dogs, Huntaways.
You must see the Strong-Eye
or Heading Dogs in action!

You must see grazing in the paddocks.
Lambing is so managed as
to take advantage of spring grass growth.

To get a beautiful fleece?
Two months and seventy steps of
tanning, washing, brushing, polishing.

If you don't know the sheep of
wool-sheepskin-fleece-New Zealand,
it's sheepish you should feel!

Trolling

Great-Grandmother Merta
ran off to marry
with the King of Trolls.
When he was killed by evil men,
she was returned half-mad.

Great-Grandmother Merta
crawled into a corner;
caressed her magic fiddle,
parting gift of her Troll-King;
played her eleven-stringed Troll
fiddle as if she owned
six-stringed-fingered hands.

My great-great-grandparents
condemned Merta,
though she'd been,
before absconding,
cold and pure as fjord and firth.
Norway folk had sung of her:
"Keen of mind and wit.
Hair star-light-bright, moonlit.
Fair face white-white clean winter snow.
Viking sea-blue eyes aglow.
Skin gossamer goat's cheese
every warrior wants to seize.
Nimble, agile, a-dance upon her toes.
Merta never will have foes."

If not kept confined,
Great-Grandmother Merta
would have fled again to Trolls,
for she heard ever in her head their Troll sonatas.
Merta chanted, Mother told me,
"Oh, let me find the Troll musicians.
Let me re-join the Trolls."

Mother said Merta's sin was pride,
for she'd never eat *brown* cheese,
greatest of all Norwegian foods,
greater than the orange-bright salmon.

In desperation, my great-great-grandparents
packed off the family to Minnesota,
married Merta to an old, old man
who'd been there long,
agreed her child was his.

As soon as Merta's little half-Troll was born,
Merta vanished into
the Northern Lights.

Merta's son became the
first great Minnesota Viking.
All of Merta's male descendants,
including me, are gigantic, hairy,
one eye short of Troll.
All of us play football for our size,
but music is our passion.

My mother always told me,
when my schoolmates teased,
that my family gave rise to trolling,
that I should sing at them "Fiddle-de-dee!"

Love in Tulips

Could I travel back in time,
I'd trip upon the steppes of Asia,
exotic origin of tulips.

Sultans cultivated tulips,
nicknamed them "turbans."
In Turkish, tulip is *lale*.

Turks brought tulips to the West.
Tulips, once "rediscovered,"
journeyed back to Turkey,

traveled back in time.
Ahmet III spent
kingdoms of fortunes upon tulips,

started a Spring Festival for tulips,
carpeted his seraglio with tulips.
At night, Ahmet III had

turtles with candles on their backs
loosed in the gardens
that the colors of the tulips

might be displayed,
that we might cavort in color.
Did Ahmet III know tulips

could be "two lips"?
I would tell (and show) him so.
I would weave Ahmet

a full-great turban from tulips,
weave my love in tulips.
Ahmet III—*my* Ahmet III—

by our two lips would know
of love and tulips.
Oh, why can't I meet *my* Ahmet?

The Waits

You deem our Waits but lowly?
Mere waiters, waitresses?
Well, *waitpersons*,
as you seem to deem
yourself so chic.
Don't you know of
Lords and Ladies in Waiting?
You've not looked
beyond your plate *or* nose.
I sentence you and Plate
below the salt.
The Waits sentence you
to kiss your grits,
can most easily put you
in your place.

Think better of the Waits.
The lineage they serve up is rare:
food with the whole
tradition of hospitality;
Abraham and Sarah
entertaining angels unaware;
Jesus doling out those loaves and fishes
("Feed my flock," He said,
and who would not be on Jesus' dole?);
Milton's Eve serving
multi-coursed meal
to Adam and Guest Angel
in pre-lapsarian Eden;
Milton's direct salute—
"They also serve
who only stand and wait."
("A hit, a very palpable hit!"
as Hamlet knew.
And shades of Martha Stewart.)

In former times,
the "Waits" were watchmen,
then singers and musicians
performing outside our homes,
especially at Christmas.
Take that and sing,
like little Tommy Tucker,
for your everyday supper.

Be kind to the Waits, patient before them.
Else you're like to wait your dinner
and whatever else
could be in store.

And the Waits would have you
remember and heed this warning:
All of us, Waits included,
wait on Destiny, Death, and Fate.

All the Rage

Though deemed by all "The Great Tragedienne,"
sweet Sarah Siddons owned a simple soul.
In short, most dailyness outflew her ken.
To help, her husband kept her on his dole.

Both men and women fainted when she raged.
She gave the stage its due of *Sturm und Drang*.
A-trod the boards as tigress gone uncaged,
she rang the rafters with her sharp harangue.
Thank Fate the tragic Lear was not her scene
(though she could easily have played a man),
for, once when Sarah shopped for bombazine,
her "Will it wash?" cued swoons, plus one trepan.

Poor Sarah Siddons' life upon the stage—
and off—cast awe. Why, she was all the rage!

Walking a Summer's Way

I now daily walk a summer's way,
except in rain,
and am astonished to see
Queen Anne's Lace
and all manner of bouquet fillers
I have paid so dearly for.

I ponder eating dandelion greens
and taking in mite dander
that would make me get my dander up.
Is wit by Nature nurtured?

I give a thought to poison ivy.
To the prince potential of a frog.
To SNAKES.
My mind slinks on to road kill
and whether I've been guilty
and how I could atone.

I come upon the splattered shell of turtle.
Should I think "carapace"?
Is it the one I slammed
heads against windshield for
and stopped to ferry across the road?
It could not be.
I refuse to let those fragments
walk a summer's way with me.

But the thought rises,
comes unbidden:
the summer's way I walk
is not the one of Frost or Wordsworth.
Is there something wrong with me?

Purple Armadillos

"Go east, Young Coyotes,"
the old coyote howls.
"The Coyote in the Moon has
taken space ships in the gullet.
Go east. Perform
for Cinco de Maya."

Purple armadillos armadilleate:
"Chow down here.
Trot, lope, or walk-only-ride
to get your Dos Equis."

Protected wolves ululate
as prairie dogs are vacuumed.
Mules and vistas are out of vogue,
but you can still get your Justins—
right next to dry gulches—
on Rodeo Drive.
Hear the duds rustle
under Tanzanite skies.
Western Chic is mucho-outré-rad,
more entrée than chicks.
I wear many moissanites in my navel.

So, cease your Great Plaints
for lodgepole pines.
The Old West, wild-if-worm-eaten,
is still in your mind. No one can wrest
the Old West from your mind.

"Cowgirls, Cowboys,"
the Ghost-Dancers scream,
"don't go near cactuses.
Get Western Life
in your dreams!"

Tourist Advisory for Yemen
(and Parts Appertaining Thereunto!)

Why did the *Rotterdam* in Yemen tether?
Yemenis their tourist nest don't deign to feather!

The Queen of Sheba's Yemen is not in its heyday.
What awaits on the dock is scarcely array.
The taxi drivers proffer, but no hawkers swarm,
though a literal hawker has his falcon perform.

Yet Yemen was desired by Alexander the Great
just prior to his being taken, with fever, by Fate.

If Yemenis want to enter the tourist parade,
they must lift up Yemen and make Yemenade!
(And if we don't want to turn renegade,
we'd best turn our own lemons to lemon marmalade!)

Beneath Meter;
in Which the Lady Makes a Discovery

I sought to pen my love in sonnet rhyme,
to obviate firefly at wanton play.

I told my love so sweet in pantomime.
I also tried again in roundelay.
I plied my love with lofty Latin phrase.
His ears were deaf and withal dumb to plea.
I practiced Greek my love then to emblaze.
Alas, that Greek could scarcely win a *oui*.
I read him words of Mrs. Browning sweet.
He looked at me at best but far askance.
No pow'r by that could I with him accrete.
My love was dying of impuissance.

Now, cognitively dissonant, I part
from wielder of but "achy-breaky" heart.

A Villanelle of the African [Non-]Violet

The *African* is not a violet.
Its *genus* really is *Anomaly*.
It flies a hairy, saintly floweret.

To Tanzania, Kenya, we owe debt
for its esprit, fantasticality.
The *African* is not a violet.

It's loved as much as our Miss Scarlett's Rhett,
and we claim cultivars, hybridity.
It flies a hairy, saintly floweret.

This bloom might make a first-class vinaigrette.
Play safe. (Don't shrink!) Put it in potpourri!)
The *African* is not a violet.

Yet, like the ordinary violet,
if trod, it won't let scent turn absentee.
It flies a hairy, saintly floweret.

It won't come with croquette, brochette, baguette—
its mealybugs preclude such gluttony.
The *African* is not a violet.
It flies a hairy, saintly floweret.

Ack-Ackery Chicken-and-Eggery, Or, Who's Flying Whom?

"Man *in* the Moon" to benchmarking probe:
"If we can put a 'Man *on* the Moon,'
why can't we . . . ?"
My green-cheese moon aged
to green-blooded Mr. Spock?
Don't take my flying carpet!
Fly Boys cum Preppies cum Trekkies?
Which *Enterprise* was first?
Strategic Defense Initiative or "Star Wars"?
Lewis Carroll's enterprising
"Do pigs have wings?"
Disney *enterprises*? Dumbo the
Flying Elephant? (Not so dumbo.)
Fantasticar, flying saucers, Peter Pan.
Swift, Verne, Wells and Welles
(H. G. airwaved by Orson).
Little Orphan Annie flying with Captain Sparks.
Jimmie Allen, the Blackhawks, Airboy,
Cosmic Boy, Captain Midnight,
Hop Harrigan, Sky King, Jet Jackson, Buck Rogers,
Spad, Tom Corbett, *Chopper One*, *UFO*, Sr.
and Jr. Tom Swift, Jack Armstrong.
Flyers every one.
(But, from my Gordon, I watch Wonder Woman's
invisible plane Flash by
with Dale Arden.)
A bomber, not King Kong,
crashed into the Empire State Building.
Mars, Venus, Jupiter, Saturn, Uranus—
and Plane*ts* of the Ape.
Moss Hart's *Winged Victory*,
Wibberley's *Mouse on the Moon*
(Frankenstein met the Space Monster.).
Hailey's *Airport*.

Disaster movies violate the
air space between *Wings* and *Top Gun*.
"Space Opera" *2001* flies on The Richard Strauss.
"Jefferson Airplane," the rock group;
Baskin-Robbins' lunar cheesecake;
Space Invaders, first video game;
high-chic aviator jackets and wind-flying scarves.
Then and—forever?
Does *Star Trek* lead but to *Star Wars*?

Whither Buckminster Fuller's Spaceship Earth?
The astronauts' Gaia?
Who's the Evil Empire now?
What Klingons and Romulans lurk?

We do produce subsonic planes with
[more-than] tank-killing powers
as our pop culture foretold.

In the Land of *Oz*

In the Land of *Oz*,
my *mate* was not my husband but my friend,
and I was *Sheila*, though my name is Lynn.

In the Land of *Oz*,
I ate *sangers* with *stubby* or *grog*
(*plonk* being purportedly worse than either).
When I asked for a *snag sanger*,
Ozzies laughed and yelled, "*Ripper*! *Ripper, Boris*!"
When I didn't know that *bloke*,
they just kept calling "*cooee, cooee*,"
but no cows come home to this *jillaroo*.
Every time I spoke, *Ozzies* clapped and "*bonzered*"
but were quite insulted when I (politely) said,
trying to time true *woop-woop tucker*,
"Please *don't come the raw prawn with me*."
Likewise, when I meandered into the *mug lair*
questing for a *cuppa* and a roasted *chook*,
they informed me I could
brew some *billy tea* and dine on *damper*
or "stop with the *chinwag* and *yackerty-yak*—
stop with being a *galah drongo yobbo*—
and wait for *smoko*." They wouldn't listen
when I ventured, "I don't smoke!"
But at the *barbie*, though beset by *blowies*
and by *mozzies* desirous of making *tucker* out of me,
I was pleased to find a plain-old *spud*,
with which to feed my *moosh*.
I would gladly have accepted a chocolate-covered *cocky*
(which, doubtless, would have sent me
to the *dunny* or some *on-the-bugle thunder box*).
So I just ignored the snickers when I
allowed as how it was all so *bloody bewdy*.

In the Land of *Oz*,
I was no *bludger*, no *blowin*, no *Norm*.
Strewth! I was *flat out like a lizard drinking*
up the lovely language of the Land of *Oz*.
Still, *bloody oath*, in that great *Downunder*,
throughout all the vast *outback*,
it was I who was as *rough as bags*.
Or at least my tongue was. From "*g'day*" to "*see ya*,"
"*hooroo*," *arvo* after *arvo*,
Strine put me under strain.
Strine was never "*good on <u>me</u>*"!

Finally, I'd had my *fair crack o' the whip*
and decided to *shoot through*.
I packed my *bluey*, *swag*, and *dak*s and
left before some *beergutted ocker*
claimed I was *troppo* from me language.
Aussie was *bushwacking* me.

But in the Land of *Oz*,
I was never *done the dirty on* or *sold the dump*.
And this is *fair dinkum, ridgey didge, dinki di*
(and "Inka Dinka Doo" to me). Still, in my defense,
only Jimmy Durante could find
the yellow brick road in *this* Land of *Oz*.

But I swear, before I *cark* it,
I'll have this *Ozzie bull*
by the vowels and consonants.
I'll just keep declining *Strine*
until I inflect, parse—or just get *tucker*ed out.

Age-Marks

A woman's battle scars are not to hide!
Have liposuction, face lift, tummy tuck?
Age-marks say, "Womanhood at her floodtide."

The scars of *Jaws*-men proved them *bona fide*.
By how much more do scars show women's pluck!
A woman's battle scars are not to hide!

These *bona fides* make her dignified.
She's won her way with more than just good luck.
Age-marks say, "Womanhood at her floodtide."

No signs of age? World looks at her cockeyed.
But he who looks and mocks is truly smuck!
A woman's battle scars are not to hide!

In ironing face wrinkles I've no pride.
As soon request some fairy dust from Puck!
Age-marks say, "Womanhood at her floodtide."

There must be scars when she's and he's collide.
Then let the world at yours be wonder-struck!
A woman's battle scars are not to hide!
Age-marks say, "Womanhood at her floodtide."

Batter (with Purple-Eyed Peas) Up!

Samson Krankski came to bat—and
promptly fell asleep waiting for the pitcher's
warm-up. We weren't worried. The public
knew this as "Samson's self-psyching trance."

We were playing for the title.
The reason for our season was our batter,
the middle of Ma Krankski's thirteen sons,
the best and biggest batter ever clearly seen.
The scouts and papers didn't know that
Samson suffered narcolepsy, that
in a game (as now), he'd sleep-sleep-sleep.

At home, Samson's narcolepsy'd been okay
since the *youngest* Krankski'd found his arm.
The last of Ma Krankski's baker's dozen
was a runt, you see, whom, with prescience aplenty,
Ma Krankski named "My Little Peewee."
In our one-room school house, both lads were
quite-quite smart. (Not a dummy among
Ma Krankski's whole job lot.) But it's hard to be
a scholar when you doze-doze-doze. Thus Peewee'd
been pleased to fire purple-eyed peas from his
peashooter so Samson could roar his answers out.
No matter the inning, there'd be no error
but a full home run with bases loaded.
Miss Valentine, the teacher and a love, never
fussed or quibbled, just kept both brothers' stats.

For The Big Game, the coach asked a scout
to come and see if Samson shouldn't be on the state's
best-leagued pro team. (Sandlot we were not.)

If it were a crime, then execute our town.
All we wanted was a hero. And Samson was

the biggest hero ever clearly seen. So it was that,
when our team mounted the mound,
pinch-hitter Peewee perched upon
a purple velvet pole within the dugout,
his trusty shooter at the ready
against Samson's coming up to bat.
The whole town knew the secret,
but no one fouled until knuckly-spitty
Oily Otis Oscarson saw the woo
Samson pitched Miss Valentine
(and Miss Valentine vice-versaed).
Oily Otis Oscarson could see
Samson on first and heading home.

Now here we were in The Big Game.
But when the balls went whizzing,
curved, fast, slow, or low-and-inside didn't matter,
for no purple-eyed pea beaned Samson.
Our Samson was called out. Coach had to
wake our Samson, lead him from the field.

It took one look at Oily Otis Oscarson The Base
to tag the slider. Oily Otis Oscarson had
sold our secret out for loot and spite.
Coach conferenced with Ma Krankski.
Her last eleven, a private football team,
took Oily Otis Oscarson out behind the dugout
to bunt upon his pea-sized brain
and learn, for all his bawling:
our opponents had kidnapped Peewee!
They'd crammed a hot dog in his mouth,
popped him in the hot dog cart,
and rolled him forth and out.

While we hunted, Peewee gulped his hot dog,
then unscrewed the mustard jar,
hoisting his peashooter in its stead.

Peewee's pea-shooting periscope yielded dope,
but the hot dog cart still rolled, so he angled
to fire purple-eyed peas behind it.
Only, ye-olde-hot-dog-cart-pusher took some peas
as bean balls, parked the cart, and went to bean
our Peewee back, but the Krankski football team
came running along that track of purple peas.

The townsfolk knew the tragedy averted
when Samson shook off his psyching trance
and banished every ball outside the park.
We won the game, and Samson, the biggest hero
ever clearly seen, received a golden bat.
Our town gave Peewee, the smallest hero
ever clearly seen, a gold peashooter.

Oily Otis Oscarson got out of town.
Mrs. Samson Krankski (née Miss Valentine)
found a doctor who is slowly curing Samson
of his narcolepsy. Meantime, Mrs. Samson sews
purple-eyed peas in the seats of his uniforms
to keep him awake when he bats.

Beating the Devil Running

The old woman was a buzz saw;
that I plainly saw.
That buzz saw, female, to be sure,
buzz-bombed right for my brain.
I ate her noise,
every fell word she felled that fell,
lapped her sawdust up.
I reached out to feel her buzz wig, too,
but she recoiled, almost dried up.
I could smell her drying out and up.
She wanted blood,
had sweat and tears already.
I could taste the latter two.

"Beg pardon, Ma'am,
would you please repeat
what you just said for BlockieHead
[meaning me] who's been standing before you,
hoping for some incandescence,
before your buzz saw sends him to oblivion?
Could I please hear your words again?
I *see* them, you see, but they're so cutting.
Why, they have lobbed off all translation!"

Nodding, knowing, it seemed,
that to which I alluded,
buzz-saw-lady buzzed again:
"But you just remember it or die buzzing.
One more past buzzing's all you get.
I beat the Devil running.
That's what I said.
I beat the Devil running."

"May I try out my translations?"

At her nod negative, I proceeded:

"Was Old Nick after you?
Were you in pursuit of him?
Was there a contest of some kind?
Did you, too, ascend from Hell
or just from Timber Hill?
Are you, perhaps, a *true* buzz wig
whom I should know about?
Or just Clarissa, Queen of Spam?"

But then the buzz saw itself
buzzed in—a bee eating its own honey,
for the air was thin. (Ergo, the lady was
no buzz saw or only in my head.
Therefore I was simply manifesting.)
The buzz saw went right-the-way-round,
as is a buzz saw's wont.

"Enough, already, *Dumbkof-Imbécile*!
Pâte de bois! Eat my sawdust!
Be my saw horse! Else you'll be,
in the minute space and time
of three of my best buzzes,
a pretty pile of joyous envy."

"Wait!" cried I. "If you'll but let me live,
I shall be your Knight Susurrant,
gather you a tribe of bees!
Whatever stings and arrows
of outrageous fortune,
I shall grits and bear them
for my buzz saw and his queen.
The three of us together shall—nay, *will*—
beat the Devil running,
whatsoe'er his fame or game!
I shall assemble, compile, and interpret
you to the lost-in-translation, air-thin world!"

Snakes in the Sass

Crashing in on His Spare Ball

Since Kevin Costner played Crash Davis
in *Bull Durham*,
you'd have to be confounded in Cooperstown
not to know Crash existed.
Né "Lawrence,"
antepenultimately "Little,"
penultimately "Dynamite,"
Davis, before his senior year at Duke,
second-based the '39 Sanford Spinners
to state semipro champions.
How he loved his baseball brothers—
Connie Mack's Philadelphia Athletics—
for three seasons!

But the movie bulled past two early fouls,
rawhide of local legend, one for how
its hero ultimately *Crash*ed.
Before his Sanford Spinners summer,
he was shortstopping
an American Legion game in Gastonia.
A pop fly. He went back
to the left fielder, crashed into him.
"Dynamite" exploded from the crash,
was "Crash" ever after.

Not a Shoeless Joe, Crash still meant to win.
The lighting wasn't much in that dark past.
On a gloaming-purple afternoon
at Sanford's Temple Park,
he kept a ball in his hip pocket.
When one got by him, he pulled
out his spare, fired it to first
to get the runner out.
The game was nearly called for
Argument.

The Genesis of "Don't Let the Bedbugs Bite"

Once we had wooden beds,
we fed their comfort with rope springs,
then doctored the slack
with a special winding tool

to let us "sleep tight."
In the "tick" mattresses of said beds
(not ticks of the bug persuasion)
lived chinches or bedbugs,

known for eating us alive.
Telling somebody to "sleep tight"
and not "let the bedbugs bite"
was grounded in facts of life,

was not just whistling in the dark
(or "whistling Dixie")!
People placed the legs of their beds
in cans filled with kerosene

to discourage bedbugs or chinches.
Visitors were apt to say,
"Come go home with us
and help us feed the chinches."

Chinches multiplied
like all the other "critters,"
were as much
trouble as tribbles.

They may have gone
out of fashion,
but chinches, alas,
are chic again!

Crabbing in

When you pitched,
I failed to roll,
to let your words
fall as rain or hail.

My dad accused
I always had poor weather eye.
"A pretty girl don't need to know,"
he said. "You do."
I didn't need to climb above the clouds
to sort that one out
or anything else Daddy said to and of me.

I tried to learn myself wise
without the wings of teacher.
Mama was no model
of any kind of learning.
Her mind had a body of its own.

I learned myself—*taught*, I *should* say—
kept my rotors purring quietly,
checked the weather
before there was that Weather Channel.

I think how it was you flew me
was you coming crabbing in,
buzzing me this way and that.

After you ditched,
I decided a plain woman did have to *know*.
(Daddy was that much right.)
I bet you, men like you, don't. Don't *know*.
It's like this, best I can tell.
In this three-dimensional world,
a plane (and all the rest) can adopt three "attitudes."

It can "pitch."
You pitched, looking me up and down the while.
It can roll all upside down.
You rolled over me, never ruffling a hair on your head.
It can "yaw," playing crab,
never going in the direction it's pointed.
That was you right enough,
though the info is labeled "corollary."

Now I know about crosswinds.
If I'm trying to land (or whatever) in one,
I know to compensate,
pointing a bit into the wind.

Memories Turned Legend

The older men in Rotary
talk in memories until they turn rote legend.

"We were a town of mills
and factories, but we had
BASEBALL TEAMS.
Why, in 1939, weren't
the Sanford Spinners State Semipro Champion?

Why, when his team was
way, way down, with no way up,
everybody knows what Bucky Hedrick did.
Why, Bucky Hedrick is a hero until this day!
You're a child. You wouldn't know.
Bucky Hedrick lobbed a PURE-TEE POTATO
to put out our enemies.

The hubbub was terrific.
There were more eyes on Bucky
than on that potato.
But Bucky was no poor sport
like that whole rival team.
Bucky bowed out of the game.

Were we going to sit and take it,
make Bucky bow out alone?
Would we turn blind eyes?
Nosiree, Bub. We fans and
Bucky's whole dugout
barreled onto the field
and showed 'em we grew guts
in fans as well as players."

Memories turned legend
are legion.

Ms. Age

She was going up and down
the Lido that breakfast,
looking for a sympathetic ear,
as judged by face.
"Would you like to see my pictures?"
she sweetly asks.
Just what passengers on a cameras-ubiquitous
world cruise need.
She stops a table before us.
I'm relieved, though straining
to hear what she'll say.

She's willowy, not frail,
moves as if to secret music.
Her longish, stylish hair swings, blonde,
not blue- *or* purple-tinted. Her clothes?
Casual chic. Green, not purple.
She's giving no age away.
She glides into the empty chair,
sets down the album, flips the pages,
seeking but not desperate.
"Ah, here it is. My eightieth birthday.
The television cameras were there.
All the main stations in Indianapolis."
The captive woman looks down,
then up, incredulous. "You're *eighty*?"
"Eighty-plus." Nodding to assert.
"You jumped from a plane
on your eightieth birthday?"
"Not jumped. *Parachuted*.
My grandson flew out to do it with me.
He was scared to death.
I was surprised.
The young are generally irrepressible.
I wonder if something happened

to our gene pool
along the way, but I know better
than to speculate.
The only thing annoying then, though,
was that they made out the certificate
in advance and said 2500 feet.
I got wind of that and insisted on two miles.
Would you believe
they'd not do a new certificate?
At least, television witnessed."
The current witness, jaws at half-mast,
is staring at Ms. Age, who,
with manicured hand,
gently reaches over,
presses the woman's chin upwards
as if closing a fellow traveler's mouth
were an act of kindness.
"It's just a thing I've found to do.
Maybe to pass the time.
On my seventieth, I ballooned.
I climbed Sydney's bridge for seventy-five.
Did you know Crocodile Dundee used to paint
the Sydney Harbor Bridge?
I'd like to crawl in a crocodile with him."
The woman's mouth drops again,
but she snaps it closed
as Ms. Age hoists another helpful hand.

By now, I know I'll not let Ms. Age out the Lido
until I learn her plans for eighty-five.
The captive woman,
raising a dismissive hand,
cooperates: "I suppose next time out,
you'll opt for bungee jumping."
Ms. Age, as if disappointed in the lady,
begins to pull away,
closes her picture album.
"Heavens no! I honor my body
much too much for that."

And off she goes,
ramrod straight and feisty.
What *will* she do for eighty-five?

Why God Chose Robert Frost over Elvis

God made man in His image, true,
but after the Beginning,
He needed an image of Himself for men,
a "persona," as it were, and chose Robert Frost
(who looked much more dignified than he was).

But Elvis was Runner-Up
and all the Honorable Mentions.
The angels say, off the record,
it would have been beneath God's dignity
to commit to Elvisonian gyration,
which would have put to consternation
every solitary constellation.

Besides, Rob deliberately made himself
the ram caught in the thicket by his horns
when he ran around sprinkling "Grace Notes"
throughout New Hampshire.
And, to offset his rival's blue suede shoes,
he adopted *blue* Keds Casuals
(in canvas, with white rubber *soles*,
which he deliberately misspelled).

Elvis sang all those holy songs,
such as "Amazing Grace,"
and had Grace*land*, true,
but his handicap was (and is)
that he keeps coming back on his own.
If God were to come down as Elvis,
He wouldn't know if He's coming or going!

And there was that time when Elvis,
abetted by a "Jeroboam" of strong drink,
burst in on President Nixon with Jeremiads
against drugs, Hippies, and the Beatles.

Elvis knew doubles (but God is into *triples*).
His twin brother, Jesse Garon Presley,
died at birth, but some say, and doubtless believe,
he took Elvis's place
at the time Elvis joined the Army.
The real Elvis came back
when-Jesse-Garon-died-
when-people-think-Elvis-died.
The one humans keep sighting
is the real Elvis
trying to make up for
all those lost years.

Elvis was anointed "King"
(if not "King of Kings")
through his appearances on
the "Louisiana Hayride."
From it, he toured the South,
made it explode, and
left hill- and rockabilly deified.

But God is God and fair.
For being Runner-Up
and all Honorable Mentions,
Elvis was made the Man in the Moon
and still gets to come back as himself,
while, the angels say,
Rob had rather come back
as himself than God.

Miss Austen Retorts

Jane Austen was not quite the mouse
expected from one near poorhouse.

Jane ranged so freely in her talk,
Niece Fannie had to carp and grouse.
"Aunt Jane, Society will balk!"

"My works are founded on the truth,
Dear Niece, and on my mother's tongue.
They don't abuse old-aged or youth—
or mother tongue. You are high-strung!

My letters speak of one's bad breath,
another's foul bed pan and feet.
'Tis true, I talk in them of death.

But for my novels, well, my dear,
take cheer—'Miss Austen's' yet austere!"

A Villanelle Against the Vilification of Grits

Ambrosia's been declared a mere caprice.
In harmony, we dine on hominy.
The Gods of Grits have thrashed the Gods of Greece!

Why, grits with shrimp or cheese is now in Nice.
And gluttony for grits sweeps Germany.
Ambrosia's been declared a mere caprice.

New Yorkers smuggle grits home in valise.
They beg it from the South for potency.
The Gods of Grits have thrashed the Gods of Greece!

Grits à la Mode is each chef's masterpiece.
My niece's *Grail of Grits* earned Ph.D.
Ambrosia's been declared a mere caprice.

Systemically correct, grits has no grease.
To *G*irls *R*eared *I*n *T*he *S*outh, it holds the key.
The Gods of Grits have thrashed the Gods of Greece!

"To kiss one's grits" is how you gain surcease,
else Gods of Grits decree it's "Grits with Tea!"
Ambrosia's been declared a mere caprice.
The Gods of Grits have thrashed the Gods of Greece!

Why God Resorts to Private Journal

Presumption, thy name is *Human*.
I abhor "In God's own time," "God's will be done,"
"But for the grace of God . . . ,"
"Everything's for the best in God's Plan,"
"acts of God," much less
"God rest ye, merry gentlemen,"
"God for Harry! England and Saint George!",
but, most, "God made me do that"!

The likes of Al "Scarface" Capone and
"Big Jim" Colosimo
took oaths of *peace* in *My* name
on the *Argos Lectionary*
at the latter's restaurant in Chicago.
It became known as "the Gangsters' Bible."
Anathema!

Verily, I weary of being blamed
for bad translations
and other foolishness in matters temporal,
including *love* affairs.
As Milton has My angel Raphael
do in *Paradise Lost*,
I could blush a "celestial rosy red."

Waxing wroth every several millennia,
I resort to this journal
(not tablets of stone, handwriting on the wall,
whirlwinds, burning bushes, etc.,
which are *public*) for catharsis.
Heaven forbid it fall into the wrong hands.
Thus it won't. My only audience
will be My Son.
Maybe *Daughter* in some future dispensation.
At least, the Catholic Women's Network thinks

Christa will get further than
God-She and *God Is Dead*.

In this journal I also report
My *private* experiments
in My private voice
(or any voice at all).

"*Who*-a—, *Who*-a—" for "*Wa*-tul-co"

Fourteen-year-old Huatulco,
a giant movie set,
Mexico's newest "touristico" development.
A boulevard will one day connect its bays (all nine!).
Now Huatulco is deserted stores, hotels for sale,
much ado about construction stalled.

What Huatulco offers is fetching:
purple, orange, and blue walls;
adobe structures with red-tile
and faux-palm-leaf roofs;
foliage, bougainvillea, birds . . . .
I'm partial to an albino squirrel,
a large yellow-green iguana
whose face is aqua.
For two dollars, I can
have my picture made with both.

And the Huatulco area is archetypal:
Cortez and the Spanish;
smallpox decimating the "indigenous population";
buccaneers (etymologically linked with barbecue)
like Drake and Cavendish, the latter
miraculously unable to destroy
or confiscate the cross of St. Tomas . . . .

I smile—
a "cathedral" in La Crucesita,
a picture-book village
constructed for Huatulco's workers,
holds a Guinness record for
the world's largest Virgin,
recently painted on its ceiling.

I smile, too,
for we have done unto poor Huatulco
before it has done unto us.
I smile remembering
our British Cruise Director's pronunciation
of poor Huatulco
in his sign-off last evening:
"*Who*-a—" ("*Who*-a-tulco") as if he were
indulging in the Army war cry.

Tuba Talk

"The tuba's oom-pah-pah is fine,
though oomph is really not its forte.
I'd not choose it to woo escort."

"Its weight can hurt or curve one's spine?"

"Pray, was it favored by Bernstein?"

"Now, will it give my lips a wart?"

"The tuba's oom-pah-pah is fine,
though oomph is really not its forte.
Don't give the tuba 'Auld Lang Syne'!
It can the sweetest sounds distort,
but, oh, how I do love its snort!
And it will never, ever whine.
The tuba's oom-pah-pah is fine."

A Villanelle Giving New Meaning to the Term "Old Dear"

Our ladies in their eighties are so smart!
"Old Dear" is now a term with more than cheek.
Old Dears themselves raise tongue-in-cheek to art.

Sri Lanka? Julia Child was à la carte.
At eighty-five, she still flings fenugreek.
Our ladies in their eighties are so smart!

Eliz'beth Bolton? Poets' counterpart.
In TV slot, she gives our works critique.
Old Dears themselves raise tongue-in-cheek to art.

Anne Morgan moves to all songs on the chart,
still gives, sans creak, dance lessons every week.
Our ladies in their eighties are so smart!

Peg Campbell has a press—a poet's mart.
She's sharp, won't write or publish doublespeak.
Old Dears themselves raise tongue-in-cheek to art.

These ladies in their eighties might impart
what makes their clique so chic and so unique.
Our ladies in their eighties are so smart!
Old Dears themselves raise tongue-in-cheek to art.

The Lady Golf Pro, Having Heard It All Before, Turns *Golf* into *Flog*

Don't say all my "dimples" are cute.
Don't say you're big on "foreplay."
Don't "golf" my every attribute.
Don't give me one more cliché!

Don't say you'd like to get lost in
the "bunkers" and "rough" with me.
Don't say you'd like to win my "skin."
Don't say you're treeing my "tee."

I've heard it all before.
I'll turn *golf* into *flog*
before you can yell "fore!"
or make yourself incog.

Don't you dare go for my knickers!
You won't be "square" on that line.
Your "best lies" won't give me snickers.
You're instantly "auld lang syne."

Don't aim for the "cups" of my bra.
You'll never be Hale Irwin.
You speak of a "hot putter." Bah!
Talk so; I won't pull the pin.

I've heard it all before.
I'll turn *golf* into *flog*
before you can yell "fore!"
or make yourself incog.

Catholic women play golf best?
They use the rhythm method.
You once read it in *Golf Digest*.
Take up the bagpipe. You thud!

Don't "shank" and "stroke" with every breath.
"Smiles" are just cuts in your balls.
Don't say it! Don't! It's *sudden death*.
Your golf humor merely appalls.

I've heard it all before.
I'll turn *golf* into *flog*
before you can yell "fore!"
or make yourself incog.

A Sonnet Upon Asking My Students to Write a Sonnet in Class

I asked the class to write a sonnet—*one*!
It might as well have been a villanelle!
I aimed at sending them to Helicon,
at keeping them from writing doggerel.
One vowed he never could in public write.
Another found the sonnet so passé
(and Teacher—*me*—a quaint and trite Luddite.)
Dear me! I should have called for virelay!
"To do your free-verse thing, my dears, you must
first conquer patterns like the bob and wheel.
They show us poetry that's quite august!
I'll give you for your sonnet one pastille!
For verse, I could just send you forth sesterced.
In truth, though, I want you to be well-versed!"

On Sitting at the Back of Edward Albee

Shoulders broad.
Blue work shirt.
Hair more than beset with salt.
No-nonsense black plastic glasses
declaring themselves and him.
He listens to the readings of
our so-called plays,
sits among the judges.

The comments of the
prancing, prating judges,
more-than-aware of him,
are more entertaining.
Suddenly we have a zoo of judges.
If only *he* would pet them.
We budding playwrights must have,
they pontificate,
through-line,
arc, rhythm, premise, heft, subtext . . . .
We must show the underwear!
We must "up the stakes." [Up *them*!]
"Oh," one says, "I crave an event!"

In the midst of such cravings,
Edward Albee slips down gently in his seat.
I can see his eyelids flutter, waft, stall.
He counts not sheep but goat.
He gets *The Goat*.
These adjudicators have only
gotten mine.

A Bray of Penguins;
Being a Villanelleous Plea for Rehabilitation of the Jackass Penguin

As Darwin saw, it bows, shakes head, and brays.
It's not an Emperor, King, or Gentoo.
When "Jackass" you call out, this penguin neighs.

The Jackass prospers on courtship melees.
Its nurseries are soon a-ring with "Goo."
As Darwin saw, it bows, shakes head, and brays.

The Humboldt deems the Jack low-born on braes,
but Jack's akin to Houyhnhnm, not Yahoo.
When "Jackass" you call out, this penguin neighs.

The Macaroni thinks these penguins drays.
Likewise, Rockhoppers paint our Jack cuckoo.
As Darwin saw, it bows, shakes head, and brays.

The blues and yellow-eyed eschew these frays,
for any penguin's subject to a zoo.
When "Jackass" you call out, this penguin neighs.

"I porpoise, hop, toboggan, have your ways.
Old Darwin could have taken me for ewe!"
As Darwin saw, it bows, shakes head, and brays.
When "Jackass" you call out, this penguin neighs.

The Redemption of Noses in General, of My Nose in Particular

Excuse the blasphemy: I hate my nose.
Ashamed, I blame my nose upon Nose Gene.
I've never put my poor profile to pose!
A change in nose would mean a better mien.

As rhinoplasty I did contemplate,
I chanced to read in physiognomy.
The conquerors are known for nose, not pate!
Need I, then, work, on this nose, alchemy?

The Conkies claim a big (and big-nosed) troop.
I cite Old Conky, Duke of Wellington;
Dear Charlemagne; not one with nose a-droop.
The "Nose Almighty" (Cromwell's) was not dun.

To paraphrase philosopher Pascal,
had Cleopatra's nose but shorter been,
the face of Earth had surely grown banal.
I think I'll keep my nose and change my chin!

Antiseen, Antiheard, Antiwon

Antiseen is underground Southern punk
and now a cult.
This band's real—
as real as wrestling.
The lead singer slashes his forehead
with a broken bottle halfway through sets
and bleeds until the wild finales,
one of which is
diving into a flaming card table
topped with tacks.

The lead guitarist for Antiseen,
"Mighty" Joe Young (Shades of King Kong!),
won a seat on the Lenoir City Council
in the biggest electoral victory
the Libertarian Party has ever had
in North Carolina (and maybe anywhere).

"Mighty" Joe Young himself
has never played guitar
but learned enough to strum a few chords,
faking the rest when the band wants
a primitive sound.
In between gigs, including European tours,
Joe delivers flowers for his mother's shop.

As for politics, I'm sorry to report
"Fallen" Joe Young's win was overturned.
"Fallen" Joe Young is an Antiwon.
Allegedly, precinct officials
made an error in tabulation.

But "Mighty" Joe Young's again using his fingers,
still playing two-finger chords of the like of
"Destructo Blitzkrieg," "Eat More Possum."

Not **Birds of a Feather**

My husband Winfred
kept a gang of guineas
that would hide their nests
worse than hen partridges.
Nobody but Winfred
could sniff 'em out.
He'd find their nest every time,
and I'd remove their eggs
with a long-handled
wooden spoon-like device
Winfred made special
for this very situation
that had pinchers
covered in linsey-woolsey.
It had to be that way because,
if you touched them eggs
with your bare hands—
even Winfred's bare hands—
them guineas would absolutely
not return to their nests,
though partial to Winfred
in every other way.

Thank Glory chickens ain't that touchy.
When a hen begins to set,
you can pencil-mark a dozen eggs
and put them under her.
They'll hatch in three weeks,
soap-certain.
Winfred taught me that one, too.

Mr. Shaw and Mr. Churchill Correspond

"I kindly ask you, Mr. Churchill, Sir,
attend my play, please, won't you? It's called *Man
and Superman*. And pull a friend along.
Presuming that you have a friend to bring."

"Dear George—or is it 'Bernard'? *Shaw*, I'll say.
I thank you for your kindness. We shall come.
We'll join the audience the second night.
Presuming that you have a second night."

A Villanelle of Vog

Environmentalists are ruing vog!
Volcanic residue bears all the blame.
The coinage *vog* was by no pettifog!

The sulfur makes it seem like Hell incog!
The eyes and other parts it does inflame.
Environmentalists are ruing vog!

We've yet to know the epilogue of vog.
Who conquers it will surely find great fame.
The coinage *vog* was by no pettifog!

On either cat or frog feet, vog won't slog.
At least it can't volcano re-inflame!
Environmentalists are ruing vog!

This vog is setting scientists agog.
One scientist quests for vog's common name!
The coinage *vog* was by no pettifog!

But vog will never star in travelogue.
So fog and smog were not enough—vog came!
Environmentalists are ruing vog!
The coinage *vog* was by no pettifog!

A Disquisition Upon Thatch on the Way to Jane Austen's

On the way to Jane Austen's home
in Chawton Village, Alton, Hampshire,
our guide forewarns us to watch for thatch.
Thatch is precious to the English—
and to their tourists.
One has one's thatching done
by Master Thatcher or Country Gentleman.
Guide and husband chose the former,
who recommended reed rather than straw;
though more expensive,
reed is quite the "tony" thing.
So, reed thatch it was (and is).

In Chawton Village, Alton, Hampshire, too,
are many, many thatched reed roofs.
But not just plain—oh, no!—
they are replete with
the thatcher's signature:
two thatched pheasants
grace the roof line.
"Oh, pheasants under grass," I say aside,
though knowing our guide would relegate grass
to the disgrace of straw.
On the far side of the roof,
when I look back,
a china cat—or is it perhaps plain pottery?—
stalks the superior pheasants
in their pheasantry.
But I digress.

When I turn back, our guide is saying thatch
is the source of hats-worn-in-the-house and
canopied four-posters.
"Nesting creatures dropped, you see,
from the thatch upon their heads."

I have no time to ponder
these thatched heads,
for I must concentrate upon
the excess costs of insurance for the thatched,
though gutters aren't required with thatch,
and thatch absorbs water.
"Because the bedroom was upstairs
and had no ceiling,
only thatch, the bed must have protection.
Though now the thatch is bound
with mesh of wire,
the wire's no guarantee.
Small creatures still get in."
"What a creature comfort," I say aside.
Then I digressed again:

"What about Jane Austen's house?"
"Oh," she said, "it is not thatched
and never has been."

The Yankee Way

They kept saying,
everywhere in Chile,
"You will see 'The Yankee Way.'"
Yes, I was embarrassed.
Even the Conquistadors
are Yankees?
What could we Yanks have done in Chile?
(Hey now, I'm a Reb anyway.)
I hate being a "Yank" "over there."
Let's all forget
"Ugly Americans"! O.K.?

Arica, Iquique, Antofagasta,
Coquimbo, Viña del Mar,
Valparaíso, Santiago,
Puerto Montt—everywhere and every day:
"The Yankee Way."

At length, we'd done the length of Chile.
Were they calling *it* "The Yankee Way"?
I was again at ease and then—

and then we went part-way-round
Lago *Llanquihue*. I see it spelled.
Lake "Yankeeway's" an inland sea
lying among volcanoes!
Llanquihue is only
South America's
third largest lake!

Arraign this Southern Yankee
in Punta Arenas, one of the world's
most southern cities!
I plead guilty as charged
to "the Yankee way."

Flea Man, Flee Woman

The Flea Man rushes in, talking as he comes.
"You called, but I doubt this is a FLEA CALL."
I hear his all-caps, know the solemnity of the occasion.
"If it's NOT FLEAS, then it's a
WHOLE OTHER CAN OF WORMS."
He has the undivided attention of this English professor.
I'm in the waiting room awaiting lunch and my husband.
He talks patter-fast. Has he picked it up from his fleas?
Should the Pain Management Center broadcast its fleas?
"Now 30% OF PEST CONTROL
IS INVESTIGATION, see."
He looks straight at me. I nod in agreement.
"All of you people working here have pets at home.
If there are fleas, you carried them here.
Fleas don't just get on people to be getting on people.
Fleas prefer dogs and cats.
They won't live if they're on people."
We don't have pets. I still feel guilty.
"You probably got paper mites.
Come out whenever you open a box of computer paper.
Anyhow, nothing to do till hatch time
IF IT'S FLEAS. One FEMALE FLEA
lays 2000 eggs in her lifetime."
The image hangs there
between the receptionist and me.
We can't seem to break eye contact.
"If it's fleas, I'll have to concentrate
on your carpet, wood floors, upholstery, etc.,
but I'll stake my professional reputation
on this being NO FLEA CALL."
I *flee* down the hall toward my husband's office,
giggle-singing under my breath as I go:
"Even educated fleas do it.
Let's do it, let's fall in love."

A Villanelle Validating Tea Parties from One Who Has Been to Kenya

The tea party is long since passé.
      "Then why would monkeys come to tea?"
The last vestige, truly, is cup and tray.

Yes, the tea party has had its day.
      "I beg to differ, make ardent plea!"
The tea party is long since passé.

What's more, it's downright déclassé!
      "I simply cannot with you agree—"
The last vestige—*truly*—is cup and tray.

I must again your exception gainsay.
      "For, in Kenya, the monkeys had tea with me!"
The tea party is—*long since*—passé.

      "At four o'clock, in tribed and trooped array,
      Monkeys swing in for tea from every tree—"
The last vestige—truly—is cup and tray.

      "To foray on gourmet grubstuff tourists outlay!
      With *déclassé*, also, I can't accept your decree!"
The tea party is long since passé!
The last vestige—*truly*—is cup and tray!

"Right" of Passage

Women of Irish descent
are great-bladdered
thanks to the bride of Cuchulain,
Ireland's epic hero, wielder of
giant hockey stick.

Now the great Cuchulain
wanted to marry, but
King Conor MacNessa was wary,
for all Irish women wanted
handsome Cuchulain,
"Cu," as King Conor MacNessa called him.
"Cu" did not bode well
as the standard for Irish men.

King Conor MacNessa thought
and bethought a way out
of this dilemma for Cu
and for all Irish men,
at length hit upon it—
a test of the Irish ladies' bladders
upon Muirthemne's plains.
Endurance, not distance,
was the measurement.

Emer was the winner—
of Cuchulain,
and of the epithet "Great-Bladdered"
by which she still is known in Ireland.

My Wisconsin Irish-descended *Maimeó*
was wont to tell me, too,
that ladies in the train of Emer
never experienced emergencies
of the urinary kind!

Daughter of the Greenie Mother

My mother is a Greenie,
Buddhistic about creatures.
The insect world regularly sends out this word,
tom-tom-rubbed by legs,
wings working as semaphores.
Each year we're treated to a different infestation.

My mother says of the invading ladybugs:
"They're looking for a place to winter.
We lack cliffs with homey cracks.
They're substituting our south-facing side.
They eat aphids, so farmers need no pesticides.
The ladybugs bring blessings, luck,
tracings of wedding glove, prophecies of mate."

She isn't upset when our cats
claw the drywall to catch them;
the yellowish liquid from their leg glands
stains and odors our lair;
they occasionally nip.
"They just want to hibernate. If they die inside,
bad bugs will come for them.
We must preserve the ladybugs till spring."
She buys plastic juice containers,
has us gently load them,
put in dampened paper towels,
store them in the garage refrigerator.
We add new water each week,
feed them half-raisins,
have learned they don't like the golden.
Now ladybugs and golden raisins
have become my science project,
and I'm known as "the daughter of
the Greenie mother who's
replacing Soccer Moms"!

My mom and I have a special relationship,
and I wouldn't trade her, but
once in a while,
I think she's a little bit strange.

Of Taste and Aftertaste

The young, soft-shoe shuffle of smiling,
white-coated, white-gloved Adonises
prancing in to proffer paprikaed rolls
décolletage a-float on white clouds of cloth,
chests rising still in oven-song.
Butter in the fluted dish; margarine (horrors!) in the plain.

Unrelentingly, Soup à la Mexican,
orange-red-brown and thin for such fat exhalations,
redolents:
minced jalapeña with hotter peppers at higher powers;
bites of softening tortilla circling a central island of sour cream.

Entr'course, the bouquet of wine,
the sorbet on-the-astringent.

A mélange of strawberries and blueberries
ringing a cream-cheese face,
its raspberry mouth redly-haired in embarrassment.
Red-cum-orangescald of lobster in suspended animation.
Fringe of gullible-green primping parsley.
Lemon icebergs of jealous yellow, one-curled from each half-rind.
A pristine white schooner-platter:
attendant dories ferrying tender-crisp broccolied-carrots
reeling eater in with their wheel of color.

Guests straining to take a gander at the individual Grand Marnier
Soufflés
peeping from under their blankets of powdered sugar.
The only faux pas of the evening meal:
each exasperated waiter-de gasps
as the spoons dive before he's had time to stab that fluffing surface
and pour in the sauce to flood the wound.
Expensive squares of chocolate circling the table last.

At home in their cabins,
stomachs swathe in
cheap-panties-pink
Pepto Bismol.

Fishing for Soul

We should have camped, but we'd been told
you couldn't pound tent pegs
in Krk Island's rocky ground.
We engage a guide for three days.
Josip senses we are not devout,
suggests a "fish picnic" by boat
our first time out,
upon which he talks non-stop.
"Loaves and fishes," "fishers of men,"
"Jonah and the whale,"
"leviathan upon a hook . . . ."
He thinks he's another Simon Peter,
and he's caught us for the day.
We wish the bura wind would
whip up a greater gale to shut him down.

We catch fish a-plenty
of the ordinary kind and early on,
but Josip is after soul.
The crew, we think, smiles knowingly.
Our excitement at our catch drowns Josip out.
We stay aboard for our fresh fish lunch,
with local *Zlahtina* wine,
then make three swimming stops,
observe the red coral around Plavnik Island.
On the second day, Josip deigns to show us
the baths of *pagan* Rome. Their hypocaust,
a heating system underground, is now underneath—
"Thanks to God!"—a cathedral.
We spend too much time
before the first column
next to the apse of Krk Cathedral.
Its carving of two birds eating a fish
is definitely not *pagan*, "Thanks to God!"
Josip would like for us to go to mass,

but we decline,
offer to wait for him.
He does not take that bait.
We beg to be taken to the coastal part off which
Mark Antony fought Octavian.
But this is "pagan" history.
Josip substitutes the village of Vrbnik,
where the priests kept
the Glagolitic language alive.
Josip does not say priesthood
was an escape from serving
as oarsmen on Venetian galleys.

I try another tack.
Does Josip know Simeon Roksandic's
statue *Fisherman with Snake* in Zagreb?
How about the Petar Hektorovic poem,
"Fishing and Fishermen's Chat"?
Josip's English goes swimmingly—away.

On the third day,
we tell Josip we are sorry
but must leave early.
"Come back in July and August
for the Summer Festival!
Krk Kastel has concerts, dances, and plays.
Come July 4. That's the Feast Day
of Sveti Kvirin, Krk's patron saint."
"Does he have anything
to do with fish?" my husband yells
as he drives the car fast away for Krk Bridge.
"Cool it!" I say. "We're lucky
we're escaping Krk unscaled."
Now we take our fish in fish capsules.

Two-Tupping

I met Prim Priscilla, who softly said,
and promptly, "I sell Tuppingware."
"Not *Tupper*ware?" I asked her.
When she, rock-hard, renounced the latter,
I *Mullensed* all over, inquired if she were,
alas, acquainted with Mrs. Malaprop,
proprietress of Alden Trees.
"No," Prim Priscilla proclamated.
"Tuppingware's so good, it needs
neither props nor wood! It's compact.
My John's the cooper.
You can be victualed from it."

Accepting said genealogy,
I asked Prim Priscilla next if,
perchance, she plied a Plymouth.
When Prim Priscilla disavowed that voyager
as Puritanical, I inferred she knew
the lineage of *tup*, which,
à la Tinker to Evers to Chance
(and "Who's on first?") is vintage
Shakespeare to Iago to Othello.
(I feel noblessed obliged to say:
Prissy Priscilla sells Tuppingware,
not *tups*, as you should know
from the "Prim" in her nomenclature.)
I've not met Priscilla's husband,
though I devoutly believe
she was able to decide between
John Alden and Miles Standish
not by their letter-writing (or lack thereof),
two-tupping accosting repute and pocketbook.

Priscilla's case would likely
immerse Iago, smother Othello in doubt.

It doth leave me wondering, viz.
and, aye, to wit: Doth Priscilla have
Miles to go before she sleeps?
Why is Priscilla so Standish-offish,
notably about her Tuppingware?

"Priscilla," I said in parting, bypassing "Prim,"
"May your tuppingwaring flower!"

Southern Showdown in New York

The "poor man's Henry Flagler"—Henry Plant.
His prayer: "No longer being 'Flaglered' live!"
(Sup*Plant*ing never crossed Great Flagler's mind.)
The rivalry existed in Plant's heart.
If Flagler ruled the East, he'd rule the West—
combine all Western littoral short lines;
erect resorts, railroads, steamships, and more
into a Transportation Empire vast.
Inferior no more would then be Plant,
old Flagler's glitter ceasing bright to shine!

The showdown clock sounds madly in Plant's brain.
Though driving for success, he eyes his chance.
Where can he Flagler meet, in public flay?

Delmonico's is their corral by Fate,
a New York restaurant with Flagler's pomp.
Now Henry Bradley Plant will have his chance.
Oblivious, the Greater Henry leaves
as Henry B. arrives and spies his foe.
Oh, let showdown of East and West begin!
Our Plant accosts his famous Flagler foe.
"Good evening, now, Friend Flagler. Could you tell
me now, my friend, where is this place 'Palm Beach'?"
"Why, finest evening to you, Dear Friend Plant.
In answer to your query, Dear Friend Plant,
just watch the crowds, Friend Plant. Just watch the crowds!
The crowds you follow, and you'll see Palm Beach!"
Poor Plant, to have thus foiled his showdown plans.

Atlantic Coast Line soon sup*Plant*ed Plant—
just swallowed up the west coast's System Plant.
Some wisely say that Henry Bradley Plant
it was sup*Plant*ed Henry Bradley Plant.

Toads in the Garden of Verse

If ever one's been called a toad,
detractor did eschew all code.
To call a toad a toad? No ode!
Toads need a hopping, hoping verse.

A toad by any other name?
Antonio Banderas Toad?
If sure I were, I'd such proclaim.
Toads need a hopping, hoping name.

We praise Great Cromwell warts and all,
considering the source St. Paul,
though toad's non-Puritanical.
Toad needs warts chapter with its verse.

Why is toad object of such scorn
as clump whom warts and tongue adorn?
Its voice croaks a fair "Good morn!"
Toad needs a hyping poet's horn.

To be or not to be a toad
is not quite right for blank verse mode.
(I've never met a *Danish* toad.)
Toad needs splendiferous epode.

I'm sure that I would rather kiss
a dainty toad than cockatrice.
The toad's from biogenesis.
Toad needs Sweet Verse's princely kiss.

If some mad poet should elect
before the toad to genuflect,
her toadying is not abject:
her verse needs theme to vivisect.

A Cheesy Kyrielle

In Eden, you'd be Edam's mate.
As proud as Stilton all my plate
with Parmesan to Feta Kate—
if life were cheese and I a mouse!

I'd sell myself as a Swiss guard.
Debris of Brie we'd use as lard.
We'd serve Limburger on our chard—
if life were cheese and I a mouse!

The Gorgon Zola's after me!
My teddy? Camembert, *mais oui*.
I'd dance Havarti with full glee—
if life were cheese and I a mouse!

This Jack would live in Monterey,
raclette Fontina Dam each May.
Why, I'd love Bleu[s], for Cream I'd pray—
if life were cheese and I a mouse!

A Resolution Upon Pantyhose by the Right-Handed Woman Whose Right Wrist Is Broken

I pull, I puff, I chug, I chuff,
exposing more than I enclose.
I almost fall upon my duff.
My pantyhose just decompose.

At length comes rhythm to each huff.
I'll bide my time in pose of doze.
I'll call these pantyhose's bluff.
My wrist will not my legs disclose!

I reach to right and jerk hose-stuff.
My good hand slips and hits my nose!
Resulting holes are left to luff.
My words are non-poetic prose.

I twist my one good wrist. I'm gruff.
Why can't I go without these hose?
Legs with no *L'eggs*! I'll strut my stuff
in trouser socks and wear long clothes!

Hamlet in Las Vegas

Las Vegas boasts New York, New York.
The Luxor pyramid lurks there.
Excalibur means more than sword.
Las Vegas! So vagarious.

White lions now extinct at home—
in Timbavati—thrive and mix
with Royal Tigers also white.
Las Vegas! So vagarious.

Divorce or wed; do both at once.
Step forth a millionaire or lose
and go to live among cacti.
Las Vegas! So vagarious.

Go blind from neon or the heat.
To one more buffet belly-up.
You're in Lap Land: lap drink, lap-dance!
Las Vegas! So vagarious.

The Rat Pack, Liberace, all
past greats, with Elvis, still are seen,
along with climbing stars and climbed.
Las Vegas! So vagarious.

There's medieval castle fit
for Hamlet's father's ghost and queen.
Streams sing and dance to "Willow," too.
Las Vegas! So vagarious.

Horatio can't comprehend
the creatures; Disney they're beyond.
They make Prince Hamlet hesitate.
Las Vegas! So vagarious.

The doge's palace rises high;
it's graced with gondoliers, but where's
the Dane? Oh, yes, Madame Tussaud's.
Las Vegas! So vagarious.

When My British Friend Bayed, Paradoxically, for Mister Fox

My British friend is standard orthodox:
cravat and spats, stiff upper lip, bandbox.
He dotes on roses, thinks that phlox bring pox.
Big-hearted, he's not lummox or an ox.
As for The Chase, I find a paradox:
his chant is, "Run, run, run, run, Mister Fox."

How does such sympathy affect the fox?
I think it's not, for houndsmen, orthodox.
Why is your hunt cry such a paradox?
Should not you go to ground in strict bandbox?
In china shops, there's suddenly an ox?
Confess your motive, or be cursed with pox!

You think a fox, like phlox, can cause the pox?
Aesop said no such thing of Mister Fox.
You might as well, for grapes, condemn the ox.
Come now, Friend Thomas, be more orthodox!
I'm sure I hear a squeak in your bandbox.
No other Brit is such a paradox.

To cheer both hounds and fox is paradox.
A *vox* for fox is less in vogue than pox!
Pull out another trick from your bandbox.
You put this hen house on, you sly old fox.
You really are plain-flour orthodox.
So why should I confront you, Patient Ox?

While I eat lox, you yoke the fox with ox.
It's *ox*ymoron *and* a paradox!
A brainy-brawny fox? Not orthodox.
Next say, "Hounds kill the fox to kill the pox."
You've made a menace of Reynard the Fox.
Madame won't have fox fur in her bandbox!

Tricks-up-the-sleeve you store in your bandbox:
through needle's eye walk camel and fat ox;
a not-attractive woman's called a "fox."
Why is your every line a paradox?
On you, with hounds *and* fox, I bid the pox!

Royal Flush

Our line-dance club just happened to perform
before the Sultan in a thunderstorm.
We entered thus the Palace of Brunei.
To gain admission is not apple pie.

The bathrooms? Lapis lazuli and gold!
To find the hole required us to be bold.
The "throne" was hidden in a golden chest.
The quest was much like climbing Everest.

When we at length—blush—found the place of gush,
we were rewarded with a royal flush.
A sandalwood scent rose behind the swoosh.
Our most acclaimed line dance? Why, "The Tush Push"!

Barbie's Mother Calls Home

Barbie, calm down, calm down.
Barbie, if you don't cool it, I am going to hang up.
There, that's better. . . . Yes, this really is
your very own mother, Venetia E. Serious.
What *is* the problem now, my dear? . . .
I see. *Two* problems.
One with me and one with Ken.
Well, since I never have problems—
the *E* is for "Excellent," after all—
let's begin with my son-in-law.
I see. My dear, my dear, of course
Ken wasn't deliberately
trying to upstage you. [He knows better.]
In the words of your generation, Dear, get a life!
Now for the *alleged* problem with me.
No, I am *not* in my second childhood.
As you very well know,
because of your ex-father, I had you
before I was scarcely out
of my first—and *only*—childhood.
But whatever did I say in my fax to give you
such an impression? . . .
Well, for Heaven's sake, in Bora Bora,
I most certainly *did* trade
a pig for ten coconuts and dance
the tango on my hands.
And the latter certainly *did*
draw spectators from neighboring islands.
Trading is a *cultural* thing, Barbie, and
assembling the outfits for "Barbie Does Bora Bora"
was no small feat. . . . What?
Oh, my darling daughter,
you will remain, in spite of all I can do, a bit wooden.
It was your ex-father's legacy.
Those were puns, Dearest Child. Puns.

Snakes in the Sass

At the Nong Nooch Culture and Elephant Show,
I *did* meet a cute mahout and take him to tea,
and I *did* call him *Mahout*ma Gandhi,
and I *did* refer to his "*Howdah* Doody."
The proper way to ride an elephant, Barbie,
is sitting in its howdah.
There now, feeling better? . . .
Good. And this will make you feel even better.
You should be receiving, momentarily,
"Barbie Does Batik," "Barbie Does Silk,"
and "Barbie Does Drums and Gongs."
Isn't that just *gong*zo?
But I hear *Mahout*ma Gandhi calling, Dear.
Have to run. Love to Ken.

Mary Lynn Veach Sadler

(Dr.) Lynn Veach Sadler grew up in the Friendship community near Warsaw (Duplin County), where her family still runs Veach Lumber Company. She attended Warsaw schools through her junior year and was graduated from Sanford Central High School as Co-Valedictorian with Eddie Mendenhall. Her husband, Dr. Emory Sadler, a psychologist, is a native of Kenansville (also in Duplin County). They have traveled around the world five times, with Lynn writing all the way.

Lynn has a B.A. (Magna Cum Laude, Honors, Phi Beta Kappa) from Duke and an M.A. and a Ph.D. (Phi Kappa Phi) from the University of Illinois, with postdoctoral study at UCLA and Balliol College, Oxford. She taught at Agnes Scott College, Drake University, and A&T State University and was Director of the Division of Humanities at Bennett College, where she set up what is thought to be the first *micro*computer laboratory in the country for teaching writing. She pioneered in computer-assisted composition, coined the term, and published the first journal in the field (done with desktop publishing). As Vice President of Academic Affairs at Methodist College, she originated the first conference on academic computing in North Carolina. She was formerly a college president in Vermont. She has won an Extraordinary Undergraduate Teaching Award and received a civil rights award from Methodist College's Black Student Movement; the Distinguished Women of North Carolina Award for education (1992); and the Paul Jehu Barringer, Jr. and Sr., Award for Exceptional Service to the History of the State from the North Carolina Society of Historians (2004). She was Visiting Distinguished Scholar in the "Educational Leadership for a Competitive America" seminar of the United States Office of Personnel Management (1992), presented at the First International Milton Symposium in England, and was Director of a National Endowment for the Humanities Summer Seminar for College Teachers on "The Novel of Slave Unrest" held at Bennett College. One of her former Bennett students was responsible for her 2010 selection for the National Women's Hall of Fame. Her academic publications include five books and some sixty-eight articles, and she has edited nineteen books/proceedings and three national journals. She edits *Footnotes*, the journal of the Duplin County Historical Society, and writes the column

"Sadler (But Wiser)" [on Lee County history] for the on-line newspaper, *Lee County Star-Tribune* [http://lee.countync.us/columnists]. Lynn now works full-time as a creative writer and an editor.

The chapbook *Poet Geography* won the Lee Witte Poetry Contest and was published in the Mount Olive College Poetry Series (2003). *Having to Try* won the 2003 Paris Trail Memorial Creative Writing Award of the Albemarle Literary Center. Her full-length collection, *Like a Dragon's Mouth*, won the RockWay Press Poetry Award (2005) and is forthcoming. At the Editor's request, it was expanded to include short stories and will be used as a creative writing text. *America* (chapbook) won Honorable Mention in the 2006 Poets Corner Press Competition and was published in Stockton, CA. *To "Talk in That Book" of Nature* (principally Native American poems) received the (2005) Charles Dickson Chapbook Prize of the Georgia Poetry Society and was named the 2007 Alabama State Poetry Society Book of the Year. Two collections, *Mining* and *Hearts Divided: Poems of the Civil War*, were published (2009) by March Street Press; *Winding-Water-Banquets* (2011) by Finishing Line Press, which is also bringing out *Little Rooms*, a collection of sonnets. She was invited to be Visiting Scholar/Poet in Israel in December 2001; judged the 2001 Voices Israel International Poetry Competition; was published (2002) in Pudding House's (invitational) National Archiving Project, Poets' Greatest Hits; won *The Pittsburgh Quarterly's* 2001 Sara Henderson Hay Prize for Poetry; tied for first place in *Kalliope's* 2002 Sue S. Elkind Contest; was a runner-up for the 2002 *Spoon River Poetry Review* Editors' Prize Contest; and won the Poetry Society of America's 2003 Hemley Award and *Asphodel's* 2003 Poetry Contest. Her work appears in the first four anthologies published by California's elizaPress, and she is the featured writer in the second volume, with a separate book of her work forthcoming. She won the 2009 overall award (poetry and fiction) of the San Diego City College National Writer's Contest and *City Works Journal*.

Lynn's stories have been published widely and have won the North Carolina Writers' Network, *Talus and Scree*, *Cream City Review*, *Rambunctious Review*, and Cape Fear Crime Festival competitions. One was a finalist for and was published in Del Sol Press's *Best of 2004: The Robert Olen Butler Prize Anthology*. Another (on Patrick Swayze) won the Abroad Writers 2006 Competition/Fellowship (France). Her novel, *Tonight I Lie with William Cullen Bryant*, was runner-up for the Dana Award, a finalist in the Florida First Coast Writers' Festival, and a semifinalist in the Amazon competition and will be published by elizaPress, which named her its "2007 Writer of the Year"; *Intending to Build a Tower* received Honorable Mention in the 2001 Florida First Coast Writers' Festival competition; *Long Pig*, in the 2005. Bards and Sages Press [New Jersey] published the novella, *Foot Ways* (2007), and the short story collection, *Not Dreamt of in Your Philosophy* (2008). She was selected for the North Carolina Writers' Network Blumenthal Writers and Readers Series in fiction (1992) and in poetry (2002).

For Lynn's first play (1996), *Gnat* (based on the "Duplin Insurrection," a spin-off of the 1831 Nat Turner uprising), the (professional) Temple Theater (Sanford, NC) received the North Carolina Arts Council New Works grant and the Paul Green Foundation New Play Award; the play received a Paul Green Multi-Media Award (NC Society of Historians). *Sassing the Sphinx* was commissioned for the First International Robert Frost Symposium. *Coming Country* (Battle of New Orleans, War of 1812; libretto, lyrics) is her first musical. *Half-Formed Angels Fall from the Sky* received a Panelist's Choice Award in the Play Lab of the Eighth Annual Edward Albee Last Frontier Theatre Conference in Valdez, Alaska, June 9-19, 2000, and won the Gilbert Theater's one-act competition in 2002; *Resurrecting Trolls* was selected for the 2001 Albee competition. *Scraps of Heart* was one of six plays read at the Converse College New Play Festival, 2000. *Hanging-Cat* received an Honorable Mention in the Stage Play Script Category of the 2001 *Writer's Digest* Writing Competition. *War Frags America* was a finalist in American Theatre Co-op's Summer, 2003, Contest for Original 10-Minute Plays, La Jolla, California. *If I'm Any Judge* was one of the winners of the 2003 Annual Vitality Playwriting Contest (Crossroads: Exploring the Moments When Our Lives Are Changed Forever by the People We Meet), Speaking Ring Theatre, Chicago (production, December 5-21, 2003). As President of The Lee County Arts Council, she originated the Railroad Celebration in Sanford, wrote plays for the two years it was held (1996, 1997), and edited/published two chapbooks for it called *Lee County: A Collection of Poetry and Prose About the Railroad*. She edited *Monologues and Scenes for Student Actors* for the North Carolina Playwrights Alliance (2005). *Not Your Average Poet* [Robert Frost] was a 2005 Silver Medalist in the University of Tampa's *Pinter Review* Prize for Drama. Death Nell" won the 2005 Tampa Writers Alliance Play/Screenplay Competition; *Ms. Spam Maps of Vegas*, the 2006 Florida First Coast Writers' Festival Playwriting Contest and was performed in March,

2007. *Second-Time-Around* (on the Iraq Wars) was selected for the First Annual North Carolina Playwrights Association Reading Series (2006), won Honorable Mention in the *Writer's Digest* 2006 Writing Competition, and won the 2008 Judith Siegel Pearson Award at Wayne State University. *The Fourth Indian* was chosen for the 2008 ARTS/West Appalachian New Play Festival. *Boo Radley and The Village People* is being offered in PlaySlam for Schools by Boston's Another Country Productions. <u>Who Is *The Outlaw* of Yester-Year?</u> was performed (March, 2011) in Canada by Flush Ink Productions.

Locally, Lynn was President of the Lee County Council on Women and Arts Council, was on the Library Board, and is a member of the Sanford Rotary Club. She has edited a book on the Endor Iron Furnace and chaired the 2007 Lee County Centennial, for which she wrote three plays and edited three books: *In Celebration of the 2007 Centennial of Lee County: A Collection of Historical Articles and Creative Works*, *The Lee County 2007 Centennial Calendar of Events,* and the Lee County Centennial Historical Calendar (*A Calendar in Honor of Lee County's History and People*). She was Grand Marshal of the 2007 Jaycees Christmas Parade and loves to cook and, especially, to DANCE.

Dr. Sadler gives readings of her poetry and fiction around the country and likes to write plays (and other works) on commission.

Snakes in the Sass: Acknowledgments

"Garden of Punlips." First Place, Katherine Kennedy McIntyre Light Verse Award, North Carolina Poetry Society Adult Contests, 2003. *Pinesong Awards 2003*, 39 (2003): 39. *HA!* In press.

"Mr. Frost's Foul Fowling Piece." *Between the Lines: A Book of Words, Poetry Festival Chapbook*, 2009. Wilmington: Cape Fear Poetry Foundation, 2009. Unnumbered. As "Robert Frost's Foul Fowling Piece," First Place, Jared Hechtkopf Memorial Award, Massachusetts State Poetry Society National Poetry Day Contest, 2006.

"From the Quill." *Cyclamens and Swords*, Genesis Issue/Chapbook, 2008.

"A Toast to Dame Nellie Melba." *Freedom*. Ed. elizaBeth Benson-Udom. Danville, CA: elizaPress Publications, 2007 Eclectic Anthology Series, #5: 271-272.

"Dying on the Vine." Winner, First Annual Scorched Earth Publications Poetry Contest, 2005. Website, October, 2005.

"Navel Lineage of the House of Tortellini." *Taste: An Anthology of Poetry*. Preston, England: clan-u-press, ceth [Centre for Employability through the Humanities], The University of Central Lancashire, 2006: [15].

"Staircase Wit in Jane Austen's House" [Blank Verse]. *Potpourri*, 13.3 (2001): 33.

"Getting Down with the Emperor." *High Tide 2005*, 29: 14.

"Breakfast at Sea." First Place, Come Out Swinging Prize for Song Lyrics, The Poetry Society of Virginia, 2008 Poetry Contest. *You Gotta Love 'Em: A Poetry & Prose Anthology*. Fayetteville, NC: Old Mountain Press: 20.

"The Girl in the Garden." Second Place, 2004 Alabama State Poetry Society Valentine's Chapbook Contest. *Love Poems*. Alabama State Poetry Society, 2004: 10-11. *Garden Poems*. Ed. Wanda Wade Mukherjee. Wake Forest, NC: The Scuppernong Press: 55-56.

"Be Kind to Your Habitat!" *Through the Open Door* [Anthology]. Wilmington, NC: Fifth World Resources, 1999: 31.

"Lobster Choice." *Life Shards*. Ed. Robert W. Olmsted. Thomaston, Maine: Northwoods Press: 52.

"Whale of a Cat Tale: Caveat for WMD's" [Shakespearean Sonnet]. Honorable Mention, Rhyming Poem, *Writer's Digest* 76th Annual Writing Competition, 2007. In the short story "Cat's Paw to Catch Poet-Lady." *Cairn*, 35 (2001): 67-99. Third Place, Chaparjos Division, Chaparral Poetry Forum 2008. *Aquillrelle Magazine*. In press.

"Food That Rides Off into the Sunset." First Place, Light Verse, Robert Ruark Foundation 1996 Poetry Competition. Honorable Mention, 1998 Howl

Awards, *The Lone Wolf Review*, 2.1 (1998): 13. *Take Two—They're Small*. Ed. Whitney Scott. Crete, Illinois: Outrider Press. In press.

"Art Is Just Too . . . ." *Completion Compilation, 2007*. Ed. elizaBeth Benson-Udom. Danville, CA: elizaPress Publications, 2007 Eclectic Anthology Series, #6: 139-140.

"Laughter at the Top of the World." *Wavelength*, 5 (Summer 2002): 66.

"Do the Gaza Strip." *Whiskey Island Magazine*, 41 (1999): 68-69.

"In Praise of 'Juler Swan Dogs.'" *Art With Words Poetry Quarterly*, 1.2 (July 2005): 39. *Tapestries*, II.2 (2007): 97.

"Anthony and Cleopatra Have a Train-Love Tiff." *Completion Compilation, 2007*. Ed. elizaBeth Benson-Udom. Danville, CA: elizaPress Publications, 2007 Eclectic Anthology Series, #6: 133-136.

"Arkansas Traveler(s)." *Digging*. Ed. elizaBeth Benson-Udom. Danville, CA: elizaPress Publications, 2007 Eclectic Anthology Series, #3: 94-95.

"Art *Verb*alized." *Digging*. Ed. elizaBeth Benson-Udom. Danville, CA: elizaPress Publications, 2007 Eclectic Anthology Series, #3: 112-116.

"Buds Boys of the Summer Beach Make Do." *Digging*. Ed. elizaBeth Benson-Udom. Danville, CA: elizaPress Publications, 2007 Eclectic Anthology Series, #3: 96-97.

"Clickety-Clackety." *Towe Auto Museum Newsletter*, 2.1 (2006): 7-8. *Completion Compilation, 2007*. Ed. elizaBeth Benson-Udom. Danville, CA: elizaPress Publications, 2007 Eclectic Anthology Series, #6: 145-146.

"Converting." *New Beginnings*. Ed. elizaBeth Benson-Udom. Danville, CA: elizaPress Anthology Series, II: 70-71.

"Subversive? Yeah, Yeah, Yeah!" *20th Century*. The Pig Iron Series, No. 26. Youngstown, Ohio: Pig Iron Press. In press.

"Beethoven *Appassionata*." *Synaesthetic*. In press.

"The Biblical Railroad." *Inspirit* (Spring 2008): 3.

"Googores." *The Sampler: Anthology of the Alabama State Poetry Society*, 37 (Fall 2005): 28.

"Bird[er] in Closet Worth Many in Bush." *Nanny Fanny Poetry Magazine*, Spring 1999: 7-8.

"Buying a *What* in a Poke?" *Digging*. Ed. elizaBeth Benson-Udom. Danville, CA: elizaPress Publications, 2007 Eclectic Anthology Series, #3: 99-101.

"Wool-Gathering." *Art With Words Poetry Quarterly*, 1.2 (July 2005): 39-40.

"If You Would Bell the Cat." Winner, May, 1999, Cat Poem Contest, *The Catbird Seat*. In press. Journal discontinued. In the short story "Cat's Paw to Catch Poet-Lady." *Cairn*, 35 (2001): 67-99. *Laurels*, 7.1 (Spring 2003): 15.

"Flying Buttermilk Skies." *The Sampler: Anthology of the Alabama State Poetry Society*, 38 (Fall, 2006): 48.

"Battles of *Actium*." *HIMS*. Ed. elizaBeth Benson-Udom. Danville, CA:

elizaPress Publications, 2007 Eclectic Anthology Series, #4: 186-187.
"Christmas Failures." *Completion Compilation, 2007.* Ed. elizaBeth Benson-Udom. Danville, CA: elizaPress Publications, 2007 Eclectic Anthology Series, #6: 151-152.
"Wild for Black Chicory Coffee." Honorable Mention, *Wild Things.* Ed. Whitney Scott. Dyer, Indiana: Outrider Press, 2008: 135.
"La Coiffeuse et La Voyageuse." *Atlantic Pacific Press.* In press [Autumn 2012].
"Misnomer." Winner, Nancy Byrd Turner Memorial (Sonnet Category), Poetry Society of Virginia, 2005. Second Place, Charles Shull Category, Poetry Council of North Carolina, 2007. *Bay Leaves,* 33 (2007): 17.
"Back Roads Nomenclature." *Exit 109: A Poetry and Prose Anthology.* Fayetteville, NC: Old Mountain Press, 2009: 18.
"Eschewing The Flat and The Dull." SandStar Publications, *National Poetry Day 2000 Newsletter*: 2.
"Of Ashes, Scraps, Scrapes, and Dirty-Word Stories." Honorable Mention, Celtic Voice Writing Contest, 2002. *The Spring of Nine Hazels: Tales of Celtic Heritage.* Ed. Kathleen Cunningham Guler. Steamboat Springs, CO: Bardsong Press, 2004: 58-59. Independent Publishers of Works with Celtic Themes.
"The Deck Autumn Deals." Honorable Mention, Autumn Poem Contest, *ByLine*, 1999. *Pasque Petals.* In press.
"The Dogma of Poetry." *Digging.* Ed. elizaBeth Benson-Udom. Danville, CA: elizaPress Publications, 2007 Eclectic Anthology Series, #3: 102-106.
"Dry Bones Rise *Driza-Bone* Again." *Sensations Magazine,* 39 (Summer, 2005). Vacation Issue. In press.
"Apologia for the Dozens." *City Works.* In press.
"Eagle on a Hot Tin Roof." The Grace Hines Narrative Poetry Prize, *Amelia*, 1999. In press.
"Why Johnny Can't Equatorialize." *Poet Geography.* Chapbook. Lee Witte Poetry Contest Winner. Mount Olive College Poetry Series. Illustrations, Alvin Hartness. Mount Olive, NC: Mount Olive College Press, 2003: 20-21.
"EVA [Extra-Vehicular Activity]." As "UFOs in the Wake for/of EVA," *Sensations Magazine: 21st Century America (2001-2100 and Beyond), When UFO's Arrive,* 48 (Fall/Winter 2010): 88-89.
"When Flowers Play at Telephone" [A Parody of Frost and "The Telephone"]. *Journey: Anthology by Eden Waters Press.* Ed. Anne Brudevold. Boston, MA: Eden Waters Press, 2009: 78-80.
"Feathers in Fortaleza's Cap." Fourth Place Winner, 2010 *Kippis* Contest. *Kippis,* 2.1 (Winter 2009): 11.
"Gordian Knot Redivivus." *Completion Compilation, 2007.* Ed. elizaBeth Benson-Udom. Danville, CA: elizaPress Publications, 2007 Eclectic Anthology Series, #6: 159-161.

"Galahading and Galateaing." *Completion Compilation, 2007.* Ed. elizaBeth Benson-Udom. Danville, CA: elizaPress Publications, 2007 Eclectic Anthology Series, #6: 158.

"Hunter-Gatherer." Honorable Mention, *Anthology Magazine* 2004 Annual Poetry and Prose Contest. *HIMS.* Ed. elizaBeth Benson-Udom. Danville, CA: elizaPress Publications, 2007 Eclectic Anthology Series, #4: 208-210.

"Tale in Old Icelandics." *Freedom.* Ed. elizaBeth Benson-Udom. Danville, CA: elizaPress Publications, 2007 Eclectic Anthology Series, #5: 252-253.

"*Jour Maigre.*" *Completion Compilation, 2007.* Ed. elizaBeth Benson-Udom. Danville, CA: elizaPress Publications, 2007 Eclectic Anthology Series, #6: 166-167.

"All Dogs, Cats, and Fat-Cat Tourists Welcome in China: *Low*ku." *Poet Geography.* Chapbook. Lee Witte Poetry Contest Winner. Mount Olive College Poetry Series. Illustrations, Alvin Hartness. Mount Olive, NC: Mount Olive College Press, 2003: 10.

"Aristophanic Madang, Papua New Guinea." *Completion Compilation, 2007.* Ed. elizaBeth Benson-Udom. Danville, CA: elizaPress Publications, 2007 Eclectic Anthology Series, #6: 170-171.

"Mahla of Mumbai in Eden." First place, Judah, Sarah, Grace, and Tom Memorial Encouraging Inter-Ethnic Amity," Poetry Society of Virginia 2000 Contest. *The Copperfield Review.* In press.

"Mickey Mousing." As "Missionary Mouse," *Freedom.* Ed. elizaBeth Benson-Udom. Danville, CA: elizaPress Publications, 2007 Eclectic Anthology Series, #5: 256-258.

"Of Lombok's Land-Bound Monkeys, Short-Tailed Cats." *Sensations Magazine,* 39 (Summer, 2005). Vacation Issue. In press.

"*Leporidae* in the Grass." As "*Leporidae* in The Land of The Last Frontier," *High Tide 2006,* 68.

"Pique of the Moon." *Night Whispers: A Poetry & Prose Anthology.* Fayetteville, NC: Old Mountain Press, 2007: 46. *A Quill Full of Stardust. Bards and Sages Quarterly.* In press.

"Feet Smart(s) in Granada, Nicaragua." As "Of Tourist Wisdom and Street Smarts." *Sensations Magazine,* 39 (Summer, 2005). Vacation Issue. In press.

"Oh, Say, Can You *Sing* . . . ?" *Poet Geography.* Chapbook. Lee Witte Poetry Contest Winner. Mount Olive College Poetry Series. Illustrations, Alvin Hartness. Mount Olive, NC: Mount Olive College Press, 2003: 56.

"The Secret Life of Trains" [Children's Poem]. Winner, The Erin Patrick Raborg Children's Poetry Award, *Amelia,* 1998. In press.

"Sheepish over Ewe: Comeuppance to Apathy." *Aquillrelle Magazine.* In press.

"Trolling." *HIMS.* Ed. elizaBeth Benson-Udom. Danville, CA: elizaPress Publications, 2007 Eclectic Anthology Series, #4: 214-215.

"Love in Tulips" [Poem-within-the-poem, "Gunning for the Big Bad

Turks," *Natural Bridge*, 12 (Fall 2004): 46-49.]. "Shared Visions: Poetry and Prints," a "Collaboration between [Twenty-Seven Pairs of] Poets and Printmakers," October 14-November 13, 2004, Northern Prints Gallery, Duluth, Minnesota. Sponsored by Northern Printmakers Alliance and Lake Superior Writers. Printmaker, Jon Hinkel. *Moonwort Review*. In press.

"The Waits." "Talk Back," *News & Observer*, 1/7/07: 2E.

"All the Rage." *Words Out of the Flatlands*. In press.

"Walking a Summer's Way." *Iodine*, 1.1 (2000): 14.

"Purple Armadillos." *Wavelength*, 5 (Summer 2002): 68.

"Tourist Advisory for Yemen." *Poet Geography*. Chapbook. Lee Witte Poetry Contest Winner. Mount Olive College Poetry Series. Illustrations, Alvin Hartness. Mount Olive, NC: Mount Olive College Press, 2003: 44.

"Beneath Meter" [Shakespearean sonnet]. Honorable Mention, Archibald Rutledge Sonnet Contest, North Carolina Poetry Council, 1995. *Bay Leaves*, 1996.

"A Villanelle of the African [Non-]Violet." *Blue Unicorn*, 34.3 (June 2011): 19.

"Ack-Ackery Chicken-and-Eggery, Or, Who's Flying Whom?" *The Pointed Circle* (Spring 2001): 58-59.

"In the Land of *Oz*." As "Flat Out Like a Lizard Drinking Up the Language [*Strine*] of the Land of *Oz* [Australia]," *Completion Compilation, 2007*. Ed. elizaBeth Benson-Udom. Danville, CA: elizaPress Publications, 2007 Eclectic Anthology Series, #6: 141-142.

"Age-Marks" [Villanelle]. *And I Rejoiced in Being What I Was*, Vol. 22, *The Poet's Domain*. Palmyra, VA: Live Wire Press, 2005: 156.

"Batter (with Purple-Eyed Peas) Up!" Second Prize, Long Poem Contest 2000, *Rhyme Time*. Decatur, IL. *Reflections*, 3 (2001): 39.

"Beating the Devil Running." *New Beginnings*. Ed. elizaBeth Benson-Udom. Danville, CA: elizaPress Anthology Series, II: 60-62.

"Crashing in on His Spare Ball." *Durham 'Zine* (Bull City Writers), September, 2008.

"The Genesis of 'Don't Let the Bedbugs Bite.'" *Cyclamens and Swords*. In press.

"Crabbing in." 2001 Icarus Poetry Competition. *Roll, Pitch and Yaw*. Nags Head, NC: Icarus International, 2001: 30-31.

"Ms. Age." *Reflections Literary Journal*, 4 (2002): 115-117.

"Why God Chose Robert Frost over Elvis." Sheila Coghill and Thom Tammaro, Eds., *Visiting Frost: Poems Inspired by the Life and Work of Robert Frost*. Iowa City: University of Iowa Press, 2005: 100-101.

"Miss Austen Retorts" [French Sonnet]. *Laurels: West Virginia Poetry Society Quarterly*, 6.4 (Winter, 2003): 24.

"A Villanelle against the Vilification of Grits." *Verseweavers*, 6 (Summer 2002): 23.

"Why God Resorts to Private Journal." *Cyclamens and Swords*. Genesis Issue/Chapbook, 2008.

"'*Who*-a—, *Who*-a—' for '*Wa*-tul-co.'" *Sensations Magazine*, 39 (Summer, 2005). Vacation Issue. In press.

"Tuba Talk" [Rondel]. *Cyclamens and Swords*. Music Issue. August, 2010.

"A Villanelle Giving New Meaning to the Term 'Old Dear.'" First Place, The William H. Holland Awards, 1997 Mid-South Poetry Festival, Poetry Society of Tennessee. *Hidden Oak Poetry Journal*, 2 (Spring 2000): 46. *She Dwelt among the Untrodden Ways*. Vol. 17, *The Poet's Domain*. Palmyra, VA: Live Wire Press, 2000: 114.

"The Lady Golf Pro, Having Heard It All Before, Turns *Golf* into *Flog*." *Wired Art from Wired Hearts Electronic Magazine*. In press. *Enigma*. In press.

"A Sonnet Upon Asking My Students to Write a Sonnet in Class." *National Poetry Day 2001 Newsletter*. Rockport, MA: SandStar Publications. In press.

"On Sitting at the Back of Edward Albee." *Best of 2002*: 56. *The Peralta Press: a west coast literary journal*, 2.1 (Spring 2003): 83. *SandStar Publications Poetry Day 2003 Award Booklet*. Rockport, MA, 2003. *Poetry Day: The Book*. Ed. P. J. Roberts. Rockport, MA: SandStar Publications, 2003. In press.

"A Bray of Penguins; Being a Villanelleous Plea for Rehabilitation of the Jackass Penguin." Third Place, Katherine Kennedy McIntyre Light Verse Award, North Carolina Poetry Society Adult Contests, 2005. *Pinesong Awards*, 41 (2005): 41.

"The Redemption of Noses in General, of My Nose in Particular." *Laurels*, 7.1 (Spring 2003): 13.

"Antiseen, Antiheard, Antiwon." *The Broad River Review*, 39 (Spring 2007): 63.

"*Not* Birds of a Feather." First Place, 2008 Grandmother Earth National Poetry Awards. *Grandmother Earth XV: 2009*: 1.

"Mr. Shaw and Mr. Churchill Correspond." *Digging*. Ed. elizaBeth Benson-Udom. Danville, CA: elizaPress Publications, 2007 Eclectic Anthology Series, #3: 107.

"A Villanelle of Vog." *Fine Lines*. In press. *Northern Stars*, 2008 (July/Aug./Sept.): 40.

"A Disquisition upon Thatch on the Way to Jane Austen's." *Reeds and Rushes: Pitch, Buzz, and Hum*. Ed. Kathleen Burgess. Columbus, Ohio: Pudding House Press, 2010: 80-81.

"The Yankee Way." *Hotmetalpress*. Website, June, 2007.

"Flea Man, Flee Woman." *Nanny Fanny Poetry Magazine*, Winter 1999: 8.

"A Villanelle Validating Tea Parties from One Who Has Been to Kenya." *Anson Pathways III: Anson County Writers' Club Prize-Winning Prose and Poetry 1995-1996-1997*. Anson County Writers' Club, 1999: 32.

"Toads in the Garden of Verse" [Kyrielle]. As "The Poet Must Not Toady!" *SandStar's Poetry Day 2005*. Rockport, MA: SandStar Publications, 2005. Unnumbered.

"A Cheesy Kyrielle." *Cascade*, 2 (2011): 31. As "A Kyrielle of Cheese," in the short story "Cat's Paw to Catch Poet-Lady." *Cairn*, 35 (2001): 67-99.

"A Resolution Upon Pantyhose By the Right-Handed Woman Whose Right Wrist Is Broken." *Bay Leaves*. Poetry Council of North Carolina, 2009: 30.

"When My British Friend Bayed, Paradoxically, for Mister Fox" [Rhyming Sestina]. *Bay Leaves*. Poetry Council of North Carolina, 2009: 20-21.

"Royal Flush." *The Outer Side of Life*. Old Mountain Press. In press.

"Barbie's Mother Calls Home." Second Prize, Joe Logan Short Humor Awards, *Amelia*, 1999. Journal discontinued. As "The Proper Way to Ride an Elephant," *moonshine review*, 3.2 (Fall 2007): 3.

www.ingramcontent.com/pod-product-compliance
Lightning Source LLC
Chambersburg PA
CBHW062204080426
42734CB00010B/1787